CAMBRIDGE UNIVERSITY PRESS

CAMBRIDGE ENGLISH Language Assessment
Part of the University of Cambridge

Cambridge English

Business BENCHMARK

Pre-intermediate to Intermediate BULATS and Business Preliminary

Personal Study Book

2nd Edition

Norman Whitby

CAMBRIDGE
UNIVERSITY PRESS

University Printing House, Cambridge CB2 8BS, United Kingdom

One Liberty Plaza, 20th Floor, New York, NY 10006, USA

477 Williamstown Road, Port Melbourne, VIC 3207, Australia

4843/24, 2nd Floor, Ansari Road, Daryaganj, Delhi – 110002, India

79 Anson Road, #06–04/06, Singapore 079906

Cambridge University Press is part of the University of Cambridge.

It furthers the University's mission by disseminating knowledge in the pursuit of education, learning and research at the highest international levels of excellence.

www.cambridge.org
Information on this title: www.cambridge.org/9781107628489

First published 2006
Second edition published 2013
Reprinted 2017

Printed in Italy by Rotolito Lombarda S.p.A.

A catalogue record for this publication is available from the British Library

ISBN 978-1-107-62848-9 Pre-intermediate to Intermediate BULATS and Business Preliminary Personal Study Book
ISBN 978-1-107-69399-9 Pre-intermediate to Intermediate Business Preliminary Student's Book
ISBN 978-1-107-69781-2 Pre-intermediate to Intermediate BULATS Student's Book
ISBN 978-1-107-66707-5 Pre-intermediate to Intermediate BULATS and Business Preliminary Teacher's Resource Book
ISBN 978-1-107-64481-6 Pre-intermediate to Intermediate BULATS Class Audio CDs (2)
ISBN 978-1-107-61103-0 Pre-intermediate to Intermediate Business Preliminary Class Audio CDs (2)

Author's note

To the student

This Personal Study Book provides you with two pages of extra exercises and activities for each unit of the Student's Book. The exercises and activities are designed to reinforce what you have studied and they cover vocabulary, grammar and reading. There is also a Writing supplement section after the units.

It is a good idea to do the work in each unit of the Personal Study Book after you have finished the corresponding unit in the Student's Book. This will help you to remember things you have studied. You will need to write your answers in your notebook. Do the exercises regularly while the things you have studied in the Student's Book are still fresh in your memory.

Check your answers by looking in the key on pages 70–79. If you are not sure why an answer in the key is correct, ask your teacher to explain. When you do the writing exercises, you can compare your answer with a sample answer in the key. If your teacher agrees, you can give him/her your answer to correct.

If you are preparing for the *Cambridge English: Business Preliminary* exam or the BULATS test, many of the exercises are designed to give you exam practice. The Personal Study Book also contains a 16-page Writing supplement, which covers a number of areas that students at your level often have difficulty with. These include: punctuation and spelling; linking words and expressions; writing in paragraphs; and organising your writing in a clear and logical manner. Take time to work through the Writing supplement methodically, doing all the tasks. Don't leave it till the end of your course. When you're not sure about what you have written, hand your writing in to your teacher and ask him/her to correct it and comment on it with you. The sooner you start work on it and the more you write, the sooner your writing will improve, giving you greater satisfaction and leading to higher grades in homework and exams.

Acknowledgements

The author and publishers acknowledge the following sources of copyright material and are grateful for the permissions granted. While every effort has been made, it has not always been possible to identify the sources of all the material used, or to trace all copyright holders. If any omissions are brought to our notice, we will be happy to include the appropriate acknowledgements on reprinting.

Barry Scanes for his help with the exercise on p. 40; Hasbro Inc. for the text on p. 44 adapted from 'Parker Brothers Company History', http://www.hasbro.com. Hasbro is the owner of the copyright work from which the question is adapted. Reproduced with permission.

Front cover photography by: Shutterstock/Baloncici
Illustrations by: Hart McLeod Ltd. (p. 14) and Simon Tegg (p. 38)
Design and layout: Hart McLeod Ltd.
Project management: Jane Coates
Editor: Andrew Jurascheck
Production controller: Liz Knowelden
Publisher: Karen Barns

Contents

UNIT 1 The working day

Vocabulary

Many students record the words that they want to learn by writing them in a list with a translation next to each one. This is not usually the best way of doing it because:

- the words are not organised into topics
- it does not tell you how to use the words.

Words are often easier to remember if you put them into groups based on the meaning.

1 **Write the words from the box next to the most suitable company department to make three word diagrams.**

~~bookkeeping~~ consumer expenditure human resources mail order payroll recruitment retail outlet salary staff wholesale workforce

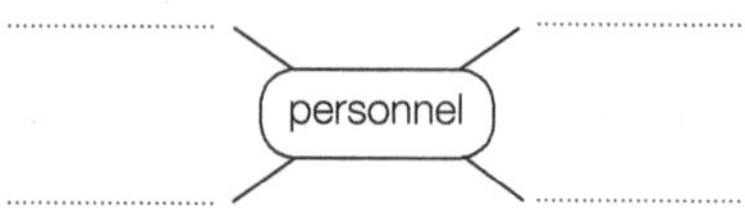

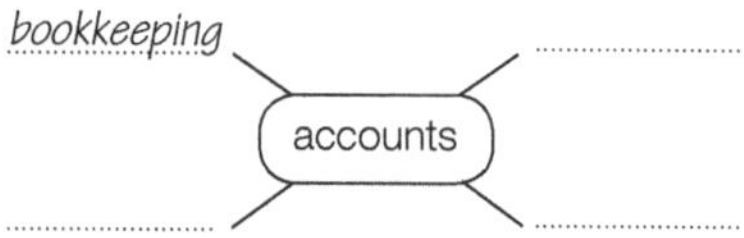

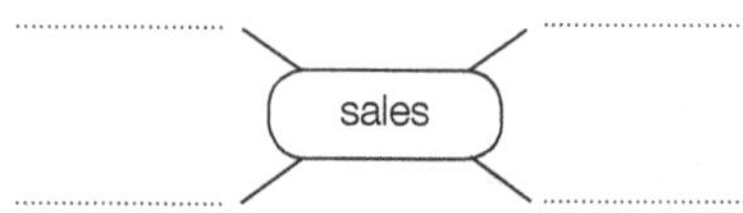

2 **Can you add any more words to the diagrams? Use your dictionary if you like.**

Another way to group words is to record ones that we often use together. These will often be from different parts of speech, like verbs and nouns.

3 **Choose the best verbs from the box to make common verb–noun pairs.**

pay install lead book look up ~~run~~ recruit work on

1 *run* a business
2 .... information
3 .... a flight
4 .... a team
5 .... software
6 .... a project
7 .... an invoice
8 .... staff

Grammar

1 **Read the following statements from a marketing manager and put the verbs in brackets in the correct tense, either present simple or present continuous.**

1 My department ......*is*...... currently *working* on a new media plan. (work)
2 I always .... the business news before I start work. (read)
3 The sales manager .... our product to be available in more supermarkets. (want)
4 This week, we .... the changes to our advertising budget. (review)
5 I usually .... my email at least twice a day. (check)
6 I .... a meeting with the market research team every week. (have)
7 It .... that customers .... the upgraded version of our main product at the moment. (seem, not buy)
8 We .... of making some changes to one of our products because we .... to take advantage of new technology. (think, need)

2 **Read the article and then write the questions for the answers in your notebook.**

AUDIENCE NUMBERS DOWN FOR RADIO HEARTBEAT

Things are not looking good at Radio Heartbeat at the moment. Their new breakfast show presenter, Johnny Race, just can't keep the listeners. He only attracts 30,000 listeners each morning whereas 45,000 people regularly listen to the rival station, Hugz. Even more worrying for Heartbeat is the success of Marie Riley's new breakfast show over on Shire Radio. According to opinion surveys, people especially like the interviews on her show.

Heartbeat's chief executive, David Webb, says that he is not worried by the figures. 'We're trying to appeal to younger listeners now,' he says. 'They need time to find us. Johnny's got a great personality and I'm sure he can bring them in. We have every confidence in him.'

Unfortunately, now Heartbeat's teatime DJ, Morgan Wells, says he is thinking of leaving the station. If he does, this will be another major blow for Radio Heartbeat.

1 *How many listeners does Johnny Race attract?*
30,000 each day.
2 The interviews.
3 No, he isn't worried.
4 Younger listeners.
5 Because he has a great personality.
6 Leaving Radio Heartbeat.

UNIT 2 Online communication

Reading

Read the following titles of the pages of a company's website. Match each piece of information (1–8) with the page where you should look for it (a–i). There is one title you do not need.

a Annual reports
b Board of directors
c Contact us
d Career development
e Research and innovation
f Company history
g Sustainable development
h Diversity policy
i Mission statement

1 The telephone numbers for different company departments ......c......
2 Training courses they run for new staff ....
3 The name of the Chief Executive ....
4 How much profit they made last financial year ....
5 What the company does to help the environment ....
6 What the company aims to achieve ....
7 The date the company started ....
8 New products they have just launched ....

Vocabulary

Complete the sentences with the correct verb from the box. There is one verb you do not need.

download reboot copy forward ~~post~~ hack upload surf attach

1 I try to ...post... something on my blog every week.
2 Please .... me in to any future correspondence.
3 You can .... our application form from our website.
4 I forgot to .... the document to my previous email, so I'm sending it now.
5 You need to choose a strong password or someone may .... into your account.
6 I'll .... you the email I received from our suppliers.
7 When you .... the Internet, your search engine will record all the sites you visit.
8 When the computer screen freezes, the only thing you can do is to ....

Grammar and vocabulary

Complete the following emails. Choose the correct word, A, B or C, to fill each gap (1–10).

We are **1** ....B........ to move to a new office **2** .... September and we would like to enquire **3** .... the cost of your office space planning service. We are also interested **4** .... purchasing some new workstations and would be grateful if you **5** .... send us your catalogue.

Kind regards,

Aneta Tworek

1 A plan	B planning	C planned
2 A in	B on	C at
3 A for	B of	C about
4 A to	B in	C at
5 A can	B could	C will

Dear Ms Tworek,

Thank you for your email. Please **6** .... attached a copy of our current catalogue.

Our designers will be happy to visit your new premises and carry **7** .... an assessment. There is **8** .... charge for this first consultation. Please call us on 0208 5738911 to arrange a **9** .... time.

We look forward to **10** .... from you.

Best wishes,

Steven Woods

6 A find	B found	C finding
7 A out	B up	C off
8 A any	B no	C not
9 A right	B suitable	C fitting
10 A hear	B heard	C hearing

UNIT 3 Company growth

Grammar 1

1 **Read the following text to find out about the history of Wipro Technologies.**

WIPRO TECHNOLOGIES

Wipro is one of India's biggest software and electronics companies. Its customer list includes Sony, Microsoft and Nokia and it generally makes a yearly profit of over one billion US dollars. But Wipro is also an example of a company which began as something very different from what it is now.

Mr M.H. Premji originally founded the company in the 1940s. At that time it was called Western India Vegetable Products Ltd and it manufactured vegetable oil and soap. Mr Premji's son, Azim Premji, went to Stanford University in California to study engineering but he did not finish his studies. In 1966, following the death of his father, he returned to India and took over the business. Under Azim Premji, the company began a programme of expansion and started to produce a number of completely different products. These included lights and baby care products.

In the 1970s and 1980s, the government's economic policies stopped many multinational companies from trading in India. Global IT companies like IBM left the country and Wipro moved into this field. Azim Premji set up the first IT business in Bangalore in 1980 and the company soon expanded into other IT areas such as system design. In the 1990s, the government reopened the markets and many multinational companies returned to India. At the same time, Wipro began working on product engineering for customers in the USA and also launched a global IT services division. Today the IT services generate the major part of Wipro's revenue.

2 **Put the verb in brackets into the past simple form, either affirmative or negative, to make true sentences about Wipro.**

1 Mr M.H. Premji, the founder, *did not/didn't call* the company Wipro Technologies. (call)
2 Mr M.H. Premji .... the company in the 1940s and 1950s. (run)
3 In the 1940s, the company .... baby care products. (make)
4 In the 1970s and 1980s, the government .... the activity of multinational companies in India. (limit)
5 During the 1980s, IBM .... in India. (operate)
6 In the 1980s, the company's IT division .... rapidly. (grow)

3 Now write questions for the following answers.

1 *When did Mr M.H. Premji found the company?*
In the 1940s.
2 Vegetable oil and soap.
3 Stanford University in California.
4 In 1966.
5 Because of the government's economic policies.
6 In 1980.

Grammar 2

1 Put the verbs in brackets into the correct tense, either past simple or past continuous.

1 The company *began* (begin) in 1985 when the founder *started* (start) selling ice cream from his farm in New Hampshire.
2 He .... (meet) his business partner while he .... (study) for an MBA in London.
3 I .... (wait) for my train when your text message .... (come) through.
4 When I .... (look) at the envelope, I .... (see) it was a letter from our sponsor.
5 Thieves .... (break) into the delivery van while the driver .... (have) coffee.
6 I .... (tell) my PA to take a taxi because it .... (rain).
7 When the chairman .... (leave) the meeting room, everyone .... (breathe) a sigh of relief.
8 The company .... (plan) to move to the city centre but then someone .... (offer) them cheaper premises.

2 Complete the text with the verbs in the box. Use the correct tense, either past simple or past continuous.

notice	~~make~~	set	feed	produce	give

THE WUVIT

The Wuvit is a pillow filled with corn that you heat in a microwave and then use to treat aches and pains. Kim Levine, a housewife from Michigan, US, first **1** *made* one in her kitchen in 2001. One day her husband **2** .... the animals in their backyard when she **3** .... his bag of corn next to her sewing machine. The sight of these two objects together **4** .... her the idea. At first, she **5** .... them as Christmas presents for friends and family, but they were so popular that she soon **6** .... up her own business. Today her company is worth over 10 million dollars.

UNIT 4 Corporate culture

Reading

Read the culture statement from a bank and decide which paragraph is about the following. Write the correct paragraph number in each box. There is one extra paragraph which you do not need to use.

- staff development [3]
- after-work activities [ ]
- working hours [ ]
- equal opportunities [ ]

COMMUNITY BANK CALIFORNIA Our Culture

1 We offer a lively working culture in which we're confident you'll feel at home. In return, we'll expect you to work hard and take responsibility for what you do.

2 As an organisation, we recognise the benefits of attracting staff from a wide range of backgrounds. We carry out regular diversity training and monitoring. In addition, we have recently commissioned reports on disability access and race equality in the workplace.

3 Our strong commitment to training reflects a learning culture which encourages movement across departments and progression within the Bank. We provide regular assessments so that you'll always be aware of your performance. We can also provide support to study for professional qualifications.

4 The Bank also recognises the value of flexible working. We encourage a work–life balance by allowing flexible working arrangements. You can balance periods of intensive work by coming in a little later or leaving a little earlier at other times. This allows you to enjoy a good social life and can help with your family commitments.

5 If you are a keen sportsperson, you can play a variety of sports at the Bank, socially or competitively. Many of our bank teams travel to compete with other branches. In addition we are hoping to open our new Head Office gym by the end of next year. We also have discounted rates for trips to the theatre.

Vocabulary

Collocations are words which are often used together (see page 23 in the Student's Book).

1 **In your notebook, write four verb–noun collocations and four adjective–noun collocations from the Community Bank text that you think are useful to remember.**

2 **Underline the verb in each group of three which does not collocate with the noun.**

1 write, complete, sign	a cheque
2 take out, pay off, bring up	a loan
3 earn, grow, charge	interest
4 found, open, close	a bank account
5 withdraw, transport, transfer	funds

3 **Complete the sentences using verbs from Exercise 2.**

1 They returned the cheque to me because I forgot to ......*sign*...... and date it.

2 We will .... the funds directly to your account.

3 I would like to .... a bank account for my young daughter.

4 He wanted to .... a loan to start up the business but the bank refused.

5 I am afraid the bank will .... 12 per cent interest on the loan.

6 He was able to .... the loan with the money he inherited from his grandparents.

4 **Complete the extracts from company profiles with the most suitable adjective–noun collocations from the box.**

wide range	~~close relationship~~	diverse workforce	innovative technology
individual needs	profitable solutions	global market	high standard

1 We aim to build up a ..*close relationship*.. with our customers so that we can meet their ....

2 We employ a .... which reflects the different populations that we serve in our ....

3 Our aim is to find .... to the problems that businesses face in the twenty-first century and to develop .... that will enable businesses to meet those challenges.

4 We offer a .... of car accessories and are committed to providing a .... of customer service.

UNIT 5 Describing equipment

Vocabulary

> You can describe the shape of an object with a noun or a verb:
> *It's a rectangle.* (noun) *It's rectangular.* (adjective)

1 **Complete the table with the correct nouns and adjectives. Sometimes they are the same word. Use a dictionary to help you if necessary.**

Noun	Adjective
a circle	
an oval	
	triangular
	square
a sphere	
	cylindrical
a cone	

> Other shapes can be described by comparing them with something, like letters of the alphabet:
>
> 
>
> *It's L-shaped.*

2 **How could you describe the following shapes?**

a b c d

3 Match the raw materials (1–8) with each company's products (a–h).

1 aluminium	a luxury items of clothing, mainly ties and shirts
2 silk	b cans for drinks
3 cellophane	c designer bags and other smaller items such as wallets
4 glass	d designer knitwear
5 cotton	e optical fibre for telecommunications
6 leather	f clothing including socks, shirts and sportswear
7 wool	g kitchen equipment such as knives and saucepans
8 steel	h packaging for mass-produced goods, e.g. T-shirts

4 Match each object (1–6) with two of its component parts (a–f).

1 camera	a battery, touch screen
2 computer	b handle, pockets
3 iPad®	c plug, shade
4 lamp	d screen, monitor
5 fan	e lens, buttons
6 briefcase	f blades, stand

5 There is a group of phrasal verbs that we often use to talk about using electrical equipment. Circle the correct answer for each question.

1 What should you do if you can't hear the TV very well?
   A turn it up — B turn it down
2 What should you do if the TV is too loud?
   A turn it down — B turn it on
3 What should you do if you don't want your mobile phone to ring?
   A switch it on — B switch it off
4 What should you do if you need to recharge your phone battery?
   A turn it on — B plug it into the mains
5 What should you do when your phone battery is fully charged again?
   A plug it into the mains — B unplug it
6 What should you do if the heater is working but the room is cold?
   A turn it up — B turn it down

6 You saw on page 30 of the Student's Book that we can use *keep* + *-ing* to talk about problems that happen every time you try to use equipment and *need* + *-ing* to say what must be done. Rewrite the following sentences in your notebook using *keep* and *need*.

1 The paper jams all the time in the printer.
   The paper keeps jamming in the printer.
2 Someone must change the toner in the photocopier.
3 The photocopier always overheats.
4 Someone must clean the computer keyboard.
5 The buttons on the machine jam nearly every day.

UNIT 6 Processes and procedures

Grammar 1

The following sentences describe procedures. Change them to the passive form so that the focus of attention is on the procedure, rather than on the person who does it.

1 We update the website every six months.
The website is updated every six months.

2 We inspect the bathrooms every three hours.
....

3 We keep previous invoices in the filing cabinet.
....

4 They pay the staff on the last working day of the month.
....

5 We give discounts for all orders over £300.
....

6 The security guard checks all the bags.
.... by ....

7 Staff wear gloves when they mix the oil.
....

8 Machines pack the perfume bottles into boxes.
.... by ....

9 They blow cold air over the mixture to cool it.
....

Vocabulary

Complete the definitions using the correct form of the verb in the box. If you need help, look at the flow chart and the transcript for the listening exercise about Chanel No. 5 at the back of the Student's Book.

~~to blend~~ to distil to dissolve to evaporate to extract

1 If you mix two things together, you *blend* them.
2 If a solid breaks down and becomes part of a liquid, it ....
3 If a liquid changes into a gas, it ....
4 If you make a liquid stronger by heating it so that it changes into a gas, and then cooling it, you .... it.
5 If you remove one part from a mixture of different things, you .... it.

Grammar 2

1 **Check these words in your dictionary.**

- harvest
- lavender
- steam

2 **Read the text about a British perfume business and put the verbs in brackets in the correct form, either the present simple active or the present simple passive.**

THE LAVENDER FARM

Prior Lavender is one of the largest producers of lavender-based products in the UK. We own a farm of over 50 hectares and a distillery where the lavender oil is produced.

Our products

In the past, picking lavender was a hard and time-consuming job. Now, thanks to modern technology, the lavender **1** ...*is cut*... (cut) by machine.

Most of it **2** .... (distil) with steam to produce lavender oil. This oil **3** .... (use) to make soaps and perfumes. A small part of the lavender crop **4** .... (not go) to the distillery. Instead, the flowers **5** .... (dry) in a current of warm air. These dried flowers **6** .... (use) to fill pillows and cushions.

In the early days, the farm produced mainly lavender oil. Now, however, we have a much wider product range which **7** .... (include) air and clothes fresheners and a number of luxury bath and shower products. Our products **8** .... (sell) in over 300 outlets in the UK and they **9** .... (export) to more than 15 countries.

Staffing

As a result of this expansion, there has been a large increase in the workforce. Now we **10** .... (employ) over 100 permanent members of staff. In addition, approximately 50 temporary workers **11** .... (take on) during the summer to help with the harvest. Despite this, the company **12** .... (remain) essentially a family business. Our general manager, Charles Prior, is the great-grandson of Thomas Prior, the farm's original founder and several other members of the family **13** .... (work) on the farm.

UNIT 7 Distribution and delivery

Grammar

The sentences (1–5) below describe some company rules about the use of computers in an office. Circle the best modal verb to complete each sentence.

1 Staff *must not/can/should not* access the Internet, but only for work-related reasons. They certainly *must/must not/don't have to* do online shopping during work hours.
2 Members of staff *should/should not/don't have to* tell anyone else their password.
3 Staff *must/must not/don't have to* use the company screensaver. They can choose another one if they prefer.
4 For security reasons staff *should/must not/don't have to* download company data on to their own memory stick.
5 Managers *must/can/can't* monitor use of emails and the Internet but they *must/should not/don't have to* open employees' emails without a valid reason.

Vocabulary

1 **Match the verbs (1–8) with another verb (a–h) with the same meaning.**

1 ring/call up	a make the call successfully
2 ring off	b gradually lose the signal (on a mobile)
3 ring/call back	c telephone
4 put someone through	d put the phone down
5 get through	e be interrupted in the middle of a call
6 be cut off	f telephone again
7 put someone on hold	g transfer someone to the right person
8 break up	h make someone wait for information/to talk to a person

2 **Choose the correct verb or expression from Exercise 1 to complete the following. You will sometimes need to change the tense.**

1 I rang up the company to complain but I couldn't speak to the right person. They said they would ring back but I haven't heard anything.
2 I tried to phone them but I couldn't .... The line was always busy.
3 I'm just going to .... while I look up the information. Bear with me, please.
4 (to the switchboard operator) Please could you .... to extension 1551?
5 (on a mobile) Sorry, I can't hear you very well. You .... Could you say that again please?
6 He was just about to tell me the figures when we were .... in the middle of our conversation. I'll try and call him again.

3 **The language in the following telephone dialogue is correct, but it does not sound polite. Rewrite it so that it sounds more polite.**

A: Baron Electronics.
B: I want to speak to Mr Rosen.
A: He's not here. Give me a message.
B: Tell him to phone me as soon as possible.
A: Who are you?
B: Mr Reinhardt from the Cooperative Bank.
A: How do you spell it?
B: R-E-I-N-H-A-R-D-T.

Grammar and vocabulary

Complete the following advertisement from the website of a delivery company. Choose the correct word, A, B or C, to fill each gap (1–10).

SJ EXPRESS FREIGHT AND COURIER SERVICES

Welcome to SJ Express! We are one of the UK's leading parcel delivery companies, ideal for e-commerce businesses and customers who **1** ....C........ to send the occasional parcel.
From collection to delivery, your parcel will be looked after **2** .... one of our fully trained couriers.

UK rapid response
We collect the package **3** .... the day you contact us and it **4** .... guaranteed to arrive within 24 hours.

UK standard
If your parcel doesn't **5** .... to arrive the next day, save money with our two-day delivery service.

International deliveries
We offer a **6** .... range of freight service options, including road, sea and air. Depending **7** .... the type of goods, we will **8** .... the best partner to work with and provide you **9** .... the best service at the optimum price. No unnecessary delays and we **10** .... with all the paperwork.

1	A must	B should	C need
2	A for	B by	C from
3	A in	B at	C on
4	A is	B will	C have
5	A must	B have	C require
6	A wide	B high	C deep
7	A from	B in	C on
8	A choice	B choose	C chosen
9	A to	B for	C with
10	A manage	B deal	C handle

Advertising and marketing

Vocabulary

Complete the crossword below.

Across

3 A small amount of a product that is given to people to try (6)

5 Advertising activity during a particular period is an advertising .... (8)

6 If you don't want to do your advertising yourself, you can hire an advertising .... (6)

8 A company design which helps identify its products (4)

9 How people know about your product because other people talk about it (4, 2, 5)

10 The percentage that one company has of the total sales for a type of product (6, 5)

Down

1 A short phrase used in advertising (6)

2 A small piece of paper used to advertise something (5)

3 A person who pays money to support an event as a way to advertise (7)

4 The company which sells more of a type of product than any other company (6, 6)

7 Someone who sells the same product as you (10)

11 A short way of saying 'advertisement' in speaking (2)

Grammar

1 **Match each cause in box A with an effect in box B.**

A	B
1 Products are often copied by competitors.	a Advertising by telephone is not always effective.
2 Many people are annoyed by uninvited phone calls.	b Word-of-mouth can work for or against a product.
3 A company has to know what consumers will need in the future.	c It can be difficult to make money from new ideas.
4 All products have a life-cycle.	d Companies have to continually develop new ones.
5 People feel that brands guarantee quality.	e It is important to carry out market research.
6 People tell their friends about both good and bad experiences.	f They often continue to buy a particular one.

2 **Complete the sentences by adding *because* or *so* and the correct ending from box A or box B.**

1 Products are often copied by competitors
so it can be difficult to make money from new ideas.

2 Advertising by telephone is not always effective ....

3 A company has to know what consumers will need in the future

....

4 All products have a life-cycle ....

5 People feel that brands guarantee quality ....

6 Word-of-mouth can work for or against a product ....

3 **Complete the sentences with *because*, *so* or *in order to*.**

1 The company decided to change their slogan *because* they thought the product needed a new image.

2 They advertised on three different radio stations .... reach a wide range of people.

3 They lowered their prices .... attract a different group of consumers.

4 The company decided to market to existing customers .... they set up a consumer database.

5 .... they could not afford to advertise on TV, they decided to write a radio commercial.

6 They thought the company needed a new image .... they hired a marketing and design expert.

UNIT 9 Making arrangements

Grammar 1

Look at these headlines and documents, then complete what the people are saying using the verb in brackets in the correct future form.

CREDIT NORTH ANNOUNCES PLANS TO CLOSE TORONTO BRANCH

ANALYSTS PREDICT 5% FALL IN HOUSE PRICES

Mr Alexander Ionov

22 Jan:	London Heathrow	08.55
	Moscow Domodedovo	15.45
26 Jan:	Moscow Domodedovo	21.05
	London Heathrow	22.05

Dear Mr Ionov,

We confirm your reservation of a single room at the Moscow President Hotel for 4 nights, 22 to 25 Jan inclusive.

Hayley: **TO DO LIST**

1 Urgent: check payroll for this month

2 Ring Karen re invoice

We **1** *are going to close* (close) our branch in Toronto.

Managing director of Credit North

I **2** .... (fly) to Moscow on 22 January and I **3** .... (come) back to London on 26 January. I **4** .... (stay) at the President Hotel for four nights.

Alexander Ionov

What **5** .... you .... (do) today, Hayley?

Well, first of all, I **6** .... (check) the payroll.

Our prediction is that house prices **7** .... (fall) by 5 per cent before the end of the year.

James Rowe, financial analyst

Grammar 2

Read the following customer reviews of two online scheduling applications. Complete the texts by putting one word from the box in each gap. In each box there is one word you will not need.

its ~~who~~ with for in them to his the

Tabs4dates is an online calendar for professionals **1** *who* need to schedule appointments. Firstly you input your free dates and times. Then you send **2** .... calendar to the people you need **3** .... meet and they choose a time that suits **4** .... The system has **5** .... own built-in calendar but you can also integrate it **6** .... other online applications like Google Calendar if you prefer. You can try the system free **7** .... 30 days and then it costs you $35 per year. It's well worth it, **8** .... my view.

when up can still and about a for this

Calendeze is intended to help small businesses set **9** .... appointments with clients. You go to the weekly diary page **10** .... write in your schedule for the week. Then you can share **11** .... page with clients so that they **12** .... view the diary and book times **13** .... you are free. The good thing **14** .... it is that it's so easy to use. Even if you're **15** .... keen on your traditional paper diary, I suggest you give this **16** .... try!

Vocabulary

Complete the following telephone conversation using the words in the box.

suit booked up free ~~arrange~~ work do

A: Hi Julian, it's Siva. Do you think we could 1 *arrange* a time to meet this week?

B: OK, when are you 2 ....?

A: I'm 3 .... all of tomorrow but I could 4 .... Wednesday afternoon.

B: Me too. What time would 5 .... you?

A: Does 3 o'clock 6 .... for you?

B Yes, that's fine. See you then.

UNIT 10 Transport

Vocabulary 1

1 **Divide the vocabulary in the box into four groups according to the means of transport it is associated with.**

track ~~bypass~~ lorry signal delay traffic jam runway platform crash freight stopover take-off

Road	Rail	Air	All three
bypass			

2 **In each gap in the following dialogues, write either a compound noun or a collocation. If you need help, look at page 50 in your Student's Book.**

(Before flying)

1 A: I hope there isn't a long queue at the check-in.

B: I don't need to check in. I don't have a big suitcase, only *hand luggage* and I downloaded my *boarding pass* from the website last night.

(At the check-in)

2 A: That's by the window. Is that all right, sir?

B: Well, actually I'd prefer an ………… if you've got one. I like the extra space for my legs.

3 A: I'm afraid I forgot to order a vegetarian meal.

B: Well, they often have one or two extra. If you tell the ………… as soon as you ………… they'll probably be able to help you.

(On the plane)

4 A: Excuse me, do you mind if we ………… ? Then I can be next to my colleague.

B: No, not at all.

5 A: I'm afraid you can't put your bag there, madam, because it's blocking the ………… . You'll have to put it in the ………… .

B: Oh, OK.

6 A: I'm looking forward to some nice warm weather.

B: Yes, it was so cold this morning. Look at me in this thick jacket. I'm going to be so hot when we ………… .

Grammar

1 **Complete the following text with the contrast words in the box.**

although ~~but~~ despite however

In the past, travel managers reduced their company's travel expenses by asking for discounted prices with an airline **1** ...*but*... now this is starting to change. Budget airlines are becoming increasingly popular as an alternative.
2 .... budget airlines do not usually offer high levels of customer care, some of them have started to offer a business class service.
3 .... , these low-cost airlines have a number of disadvantages. There is often no compensation if the flight is cancelled. Changing the time of your flight can often be expensive, too. **4** .... the higher cost of tickets, the best option for many companies is still a corporate rate with a traditional airline.

2 **Write out the following text with the correct punctuation. You will need to add full stops and commas and change some of the letters to capitals.**

high speed railways are a big business in China and have attracted a great deal of investment the system started in 2007 with less than 250,000 passengers a day but now the number has reached over 800,000 you can now travel from Beijing to Shanghai in about five hours whereas only a few years ago it took twice as long however this rapid growth has also seen some setbacks like the serious train crash in Wenzhou in July 2011 despite this safety standards on Chinese railways remain high

Vocabulary 2

Contrast words and link words can help you to work out the meanings of words you don't know. Work out the meanings of the words in italics in these sentences using the contrast or link word to help you. Write a word or phrase that is similar in meaning.

1 I thought there would be very few people at that time in the morning but actually the train was *packed*. ...*full*...

2 Although his article about the high speed train was very interesting, the talk that he gave was rather *dull*. ....

3 Many traditional airlines are experiencing low passenger numbers whereas most budget airlines are *thriving*. ....

4 I was expecting the interview to be *tough*, but I found most of the questions fairly easy. ....

5 Despite the slight *dip* in sales this month, the general forecast is for increased growth. ....

UNIT 11 Working holidays

Grammar

1 **Read the following job advertisements and complete the sentences below with comparative forms of the adjectives in the box. Use each adjective once.**

SPEND A WORKING HOLIDAY IN NEW ZEALAND

You are allowed to work and travel for 12 months on a working holiday visa. Browse our current job vacancies below.

A

Star Viticulture Ltd requires a

VINEYARD SUPERVISOR

You will have at least one year's experience of supervision and knowledge of health and safety procedures. You will also be required to help with picking and loading.

You should have a working knowledge of English.

You will be at least 18 years of age.

Pay: 650 dollars per week

Only apply if you can commit to at least three months.

B

NZBookings.com

HOTEL CO-ORDINATOR REQUIRED

Responsible for hotel websites and assisting with administrative tasks in our booking office.

The successful candidate will have:

- education to degree level
- fluent English
- good communication and selling skills

Salary: 2900 dollars per month. Initial contract for six months.

~~young~~	fit	good	long	high	demanding	low	important

1 You cannot apply for job A if you are *younger* than 18.
2 The initial contract is .... for job B.
3 Candidates for job A can have a .... level of education.
4 Candidates for job B have to speak .... English.
5 I imagine you need to be physically .... to do job A than job B.
6 Job B offers slightly .... pay than job A.
7 Communication skills are .... in job B than job A.
8 I think job A sounds .... than job B.

2 **Complete the second sentence so that it means the same as the first.**

1 On average, London is warmer than New York in January.
On average, London isn't *as cold as* New York in January.

2 On the whole, our situation is better than I thought it was.
On the whole, our situation isn't .... I thought it was.

3 James starts work later than the rest of the team.
James doesn't start work .... the rest of the team.

4 My journey to work is shorter than yours.
My journey to work isn't .... yours.

5 I'm afraid the process is more complicated than I imagined.
I'm afraid the process isn't .... I imagined.

Grammar and vocabulary

Complete the following article about offsite meetings. Choose the correct word, A, B or C, to fill each gap (1–12).

OFFSITE MEETINGS

People often say that offsite meetings can be a good thing. Meeting in a country hotel, or **1** ......*B*...... in a team member's house, encourages more creative thinking **2** .... staying in the office and it helps people to bond. All too often, however, these meetings do not go as well **3** .... the organisers hoped. **4** .... all the careful planning, employees often come away feeling dissatisfied. Why is this? The problem is often that the organisers have not **5** .... clear objectives, because so much time **6** .... spent on discussing details like the date and the venue. Of course these are important, but the objectives also **7** .... to be agreed at the start and kept in **8** .... during the planning. The other mistake that is often **9** .... is that the meeting is not followed up effectively. Immediately after the offsite meeting, a report **10** .... be put together, and further meetings arranged. Without this, the good ideas that people **11** .... up with will soon be forgotten and **12** .... a result, staff will feel they have wasted their time.

1	A too	B even	C and
2	A as	B to	C than
3	A like	B as	C than
4	A Although	B But	C Despite
5	A put	B set	C done
6	A is	B are	C have
7	A must	B need	C should
8	A thought	B head	C mind
9	A done	B made	C taken
10	A should	B needs	C ought
11	A made	B put	C came
12	A as	B to	C for

UNIT 12 Conferences

Grammar

Below you will find feedback forms from two delegates about a conference.

Delegate A

	poor	satisfactory	good	very good
Irina Kruger		✓		
Rachel Tebbit			✓	
John Zhu				✓
Dr Bruno Alfano			✓	
Alan Rolfe			✓	
Discussion panel	✓			
Location			✓	
Conference staff				✓

Comments:

Mr Zhu's talk v. useful, but not a good room – too small. Rachel Tebbit was also interesting.
Least interesting part was discussion panel – too long and boring.
Conference staff v. helpful, unlike last year!

Delegate B

	poor	satisfactory	good	very good
Irina Kruger		✓		
Rachel Tebbit			✓	
John Zhu			✓	
Dr Bruno Alfano				✓
Alan Rolfe			✓	
Discussion panel			✓	
Location		✓		
Conference staff			✓	

Comments:

Dr Alfano's session really good, and great fun! Mr Rolfe also useful but a bit serious.
Hotel rather far from centre. Why not same hotel as last year?
Two hours not enough for discussion panel.

Study the forms and complete the sentences with either a comparative or a superlative form of the adjectives in the box. Use each adjective once only.

dull entertaining ~~good~~ useful helpful ~~interesting~~ large long

1 Delegate A thinks that Rachel Tebbit's talk was *more interesting* than Irina Kruger's.
2 Delegate B thinks that Dr Alfano's talk was *the best* .
3 Delegate A thinks that the conference staff were .... than last year.
4 Delegate A thinks that John Zhu's session needed a .... room.
5 Delegate A thinks that the discussion panel was .... part.
6 Delegate B thinks that it is a pity that the discussion panel was not ....
7 Delegate A thinks that John Zhu's session was .... of all.
8 Delegate B thinks that Dr Alfano was .... than Mr Rolfe.

Vocabulary

1 **Match the verbs in Column A with nouns in Column B to make collocations about organising or attending a conference. Some verbs can go with more than one noun.**

A	B
wear	a presentation
give	the venue
put up	a feedback form
attend	a badge
book	a lecture
give out	information packs
fill in	signs

2 **Who would normally do each of the actions in the list above? Record each collocation in the correct column below. One action would normally be done by all three types of people.**

A delegate	A speaker	An organiser
attend a lecture		

UNIT 13 New places, new people

Grammar

1 **Complete the following profile of a company manager, putting the verbs in brackets in either the past simple or the present perfect.**

JIM BLAKE

Jim Blake **1** *joined* (join) Hodson Electricals in 1980, immediately after finishing his degree in chemical engineering. In 1988, the company **2** .... (choose) him to run the consumer products division. Then, in 1995, Jim's strong performance **3** .... (earn) him the top job. He **4** .... (become) CEO of Hodson Electricals at the age of just 46.

Since then, Jim's career **5** .... (be) an example of how to manage a company successfully. For the last ten years, Hodson Electricals **6** .... (expand) continually and now it **7** .... (become) one of the most highly valued companies in Europe. One of Jim's secrets is to develop talented people. Recently, he **8** .... (establish) a series of performance measures that identify who the best performers are. Executives are now promoted without regard to seniority. For example, when he had to choose a new Chief Financial Officer two years ago, Blake **9** .... (pass) over several candidates in favour of 38-year-old Ben Bradley. He **10** .... (always insist), 'Age doesn't matter. It's your ability that counts'.

People **11** .... (call) Blake many things during his career but one thing that nobody can call him is lazy. His energy and enthusiasm **12** .... (make) the company what it is today.

2 **For the following sentences, write a sentence with the same meaning, using the verb in capitals and either *for* or *since*.**

1 I started my job here three months ago.
WORK
I've worked here for three months.

2 We bought the new machinery in January.
HAVE
....

3 I first met your CEO several years ago.
KNOW
....

4 He moved to California in 2009.
LIVE

....

5 Mr Boston went on holiday five days ago.
BE

....

6 I began this job in 2008.
DO

....

7 We started ordering from that supplier ages ago.
USE

....

8 James left this company in April.
NOT WORK

....

Vocabulary

English has a number of different verbs for making types of changes. Choose the most suitable verb from the box to complete the following sentences.

move vary convert swap revise revolutionise adapt ~~adjust~~

1 Our policy is not to raise salaries in real terms but just adjust them for inflation.

2 On average we earn about £6000 a month but it can .... a lot depending on the time of year.

3 They are planning to .... the old warehouse into offices.

4 The new offices will be ready for us to .... into in June.

5 They say that this new system will .... the way we work but I don't really believe it.

6 If we want to survive as a company, we will have to .... to this new situation. We can't turn the clock back.

7 They say the government are planning to .... their economic policy.

8 I know he earns a lot more money than me, but I still wouldn't like to .... jobs with my boss.

UNIT 14 Corporate gift-giving

Grammar

1 **Decide if the plurals in the following sentences are correct or not. If not, change them and make any other necessary changes to the grammar.**

1 All ~~these paperworks~~ *this paperwork* ~~have~~ *has* to be done before the end of today.
2 New jobs are usually advertised on the website.
3 I have some facts and figures that I think will interest you.
4 These furnitures are not very suitable for our office.
5 I'm afraid progresses with this project have been rather slow.
6 There are signs that the economy is starting to improve.
7 All the evidences suggest that tax cuts can encourage economic growth.
8 He crashed the car this morning but fortunately the damages aren't serious.
9 The feedbacks from customers have been almost entirely positive.

2 **The words in the box can be either countable or uncountable, with a slightly different meaning. Complete the sentences below by using each noun twice, either in the uncountable or the plural form.**

paper/papers	business/businesses	room/rooms
competition/competitions	time/times	coffee/~~coffees~~

1 Could we have two *coffees* please, one without milk?
2 It's a difficult market to enter because there is a lot of ....
3 I'm afraid the photocopier has run out of ....
4 Our country needs people with the talent and drive to start up new ....
5 We may get some new .... from our contacts in Eastern Europe.
6 There is an old saying that .... is money.
7 There isn't enough .... to put another desk in here.
8 Some companies try to attract new customers by organising .... where you can win a prize.
9 Brazil is the world's largest exporter of ....
10 We rent out our conference .... by the hour.
11 Two of our business students are presenting research .... at the conference.
12 In these difficult .... , I am afraid we just have to make some cutbacks.

3 **Complete the following text using *a*, *the* or no article (–) in each gap.**

BUSINESS GREETING CARDS

If you run **1** ...*a*... business, should you send **2** .... greetings cards to your clients? **3** .... answer is probably 'yes'. They show that you value your clients' custom and help to build up **4** .... good relationship with them. It is important to buy **5** .... good quality ones and to sign them personally. **6** .... brief personal message is also **7** .... nice addition. You should either write **8** .... name of your company under your signature, or include your business card in **9** .... envelope as well. Of course, make sure you send your cards in good time, especially in **10** .... December when they may be delayed in **11** .... post.

You should remember that some of your clients may have **12** .... different religious beliefs, so it might be **13** .... good idea to avoid **14** .... cards which have a religious greeting. **15** .... best message is probably 'Best wishes' or 'Seasons Greetings'.

Vocabulary

Complete the sentences by putting one of the verbs or nouns from the box in each gap. You may need to change the tense of the verbs.

donate	donation	~~present (noun)~~	present (verb)	presentation
offer (noun)	offer (verb)	share (verb)	share (noun)	

1 Everyone in the office gave five pounds so they could buy Deborah a leaving *present*.

2 'Have you heard anything from Samsung yet?' 'Yes, good news. They .... me the job.'

3 Last month the management team .... Mr Wick with a silver plate to celebrate his forty years with the company.

4 Traditionally, the company makes a/an .... to a children's charity once a year.

5 The company has made a/an .... to acquire Douce, the perfume business.

6 Everyone should get a fair .... of the profits.

7 The prize will be given at a/an .... ceremony at the Hilton hotel.

8 He supports a lot of political causes and .... over £10,000 to the party last year.

9 I'm afraid I don't have enough copies of the handouts, so please could one or two people .... ?

UNIT **15** # Teamwork

Vocabulary

1 **Add suffixes to the following verbs to make nouns and adjectives.**

Verb	Noun	Adjective
entertain	*entertainment*	*entertaining*
excite		
attract		
enjoy		
protect		
create		
appreciate		
communicate		
co-operate		
benefit		

2 **Complete the sentences with a word formed from the verb in brackets.**

1 The treasure hunt was very *entertaining* (entertain) but I'm not sure if it was very profitable.

2 Good teamwork requires full .... (co-operate) between all the team members.

3 The team came up with a number of .... (attract) suggestions.

4 This is one of the most .... (excite) projects we have worked on.

5 Please accept this small gift as a token of our .... (appreciate).

6 Problem-solving activities are a good way of encouraging .... (create) among employees.

7 If you're taking part in a painting workshop, you need .... (protect) clothing.

8 We are involved in several projects which we hope will be .... (benefit) for the local community.

9 I am writing to thank you for organising such an .... (enjoy) event.

10 Most of our problems have been caused by lack of .... (communicate) between different departments.

3 Complete the sentences below with the most suitable noun from the box. Each one will make a compound noun with the word *team*.

leader player meeting effort ~~building~~

1 We need to think of some team- *building* activities to bring people together.
2 A team .... needs to know how to delegate tasks to the right people in the group.
3 We hold a team .... every Friday to discuss the week's progress.
4 On his CV, he describes himself as an excellent communicator and a team ....
5 A: I think you've done a wonderful job of designing the new flyers.
B: Oh it wasn't just me. It was a team .... really.

4 Use pairs of words from the box to form compound nouns (they are all found in Unit 15 of the Student's Book). Then insert each compound into the most suitable sentence below.

~~block~~ management box consultancy control
staff suggestions ~~booking~~ quality maintenance

1 We have made a *block booking* at the Norton Hotel for the conference in October.
2 Please report any broken equipment to the ....
3 We are a global .... and advisor to some of the world's most successful businesses.
4 One way of collecting employees' ideas is to put a .... in the office.
5 At least 10 per cent of our output is tested by the .... team.

Grammar

Complete the advertisement with the words in the box. There are three words you will not need.

out down on of to ~~for~~ at the a some no and but

GRIMTHORPE'S MURDER MYSTERIES

If you are looking **1** *for* a team-building event which will really break **2** .... barriers and make everyone work together **3** .... solve a puzzle, then one of our murder mystery events is **4** .... perfect choice. We run them in hotels, offices **5** .... even private houses. Everyone plays **6** .... different character and one **7** .... you is the murderer. Examine the venue for clues and interview the suspects to work **8** .... who is telling lies. There's **9** .... better way of getting everyone talking together. Contact us **10** .... 0161 7758698.

UNIT 16 Thinking globally

Grammar

1 Underline the correct quantity expressions in the following sentences.

1. These days a *great deal of*/*a great many* schools offer training in global management.
2. The increasingly global economy has brought *several*/*much* new challenges.
3. I don't think *much*/*many* people in our department are willing to relocate.
4. I would like to recommend *a few*/*a little* books on cultural awareness.
5. We can learn *a great deal*/*a great many* by looking at how companies are organised in other cultures.
6. Meetings often start late in this country, so sometimes you need *a few*/*a little* patience.
7. *A great deal of*/*A great many* Chinese capital is now invested in Europe.
8. There were *so much*/*so many* business events I had to attend on my trip that I had *very few*/*very little* time for sightseeing.

> Quantity words like *most*/*much*/*many*/*a few*/*a little* are not followed by *of* when there is a noun immediately after them. We only use *of* when they are followed by a word like a pronoun, possessive adjective or article.
>
> Some other quantity expressions based on nouns, e.g. *the majority*, always use *of*.

2 Write *of* or nothing (–) in the following sentences.

1. Do you know how many ....*of*.... our customers are based in China?
2. Most .... students take an English exam as part of their degree.
3. I don't know what is causing this problem but I'm sure most .... it is cultural.
4. In some countries people prefer not to spend much .... time on small talk.
5. The vast majority .... our employees speak some Chinese.
6. You are probably aware of some cultural differences but many .... them are not obvious at first.
7. I didn't have time to see much .... the city on my trip.
8. Only a small minority .... people have never used the Internet.
9. A great many .... managers have to deal with international teams but few .... them are really prepared for it.

Grammar and vocabulary

Complete the following text. Choose the correct word, A, B or C, to fill each gap (1–12).

A recent study **1** ....C.... concluded that a company's overall performance can often **2** .... improved by the recruitment of experts from other countries. Companies which **3** .... an effort to do this offer wages which **4** .... average are two per cent higher **5** .... in companies which only take on people from the domestic market. One obvious reason **6** .... this is that experts from other countries will know **7** .... more about overseas markets. The same study shows that **8** .... companies often increase their exports **9** .... a foreign expert joins the team. **10** .... , there are almost certainly other advantages which are less easy **11** .... measure. An expert from another culture will bring new ideas and new ways of working which can **12** .... the company the edge over the competition.

1	A is	B have	C has
2	A is	B be	C are
3	A make	B give	C take
4	A in	B on	C by
5	A as	B than	C of
6	A to	B of	C for
7	A much	B many	C most
8	A this	B these	C that
9	A when	B while	C as
10	A Although	B Whereas	C However
11	A for	B of	C to
12	A have	B make	C give

Vocabulary

Choose the word or expression which best completes each sentence. If you have difficulties, look back at the text in the Student's Book on page 77.

1 Offshore operations often .... a different role now from twenty years ago.
A do B act C play

2 A .... flyer means someone with special abilities who is likely to succeed.
A tall B high C far

3 In some countries people tend to rely .... university lecturers to find them jobs.
A on B from C at

4 Working in a different country and culture can be a/an ....
A viewfinder B eye opener C sightseer

5 Many HR managers today try to recruit from a global .... of talent.
A lake B river C pool

UNIT

17 Describing statistics

Grammar

The following line graph shows a country's unemployment rate (percentage of the workforce who are unemployed) during the period of one financial year.

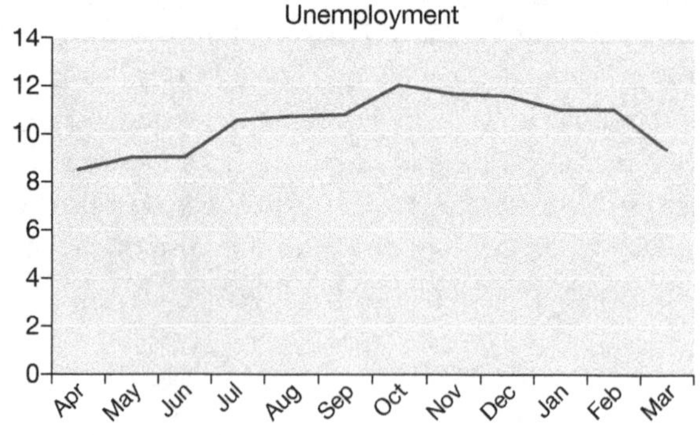

1 **Read the following description of the graph.**
In April, the unemployment rate stood at just over 8 per cent. *There was a slight increase* in May but then it remained constant during the month of June. In July *it rose sharply* to over 10 per cent. From July to September, *there was a very gradual rise* but in October *it rose more steeply* to reach 12 per cent. After that, however, *it declined gradually* until January. At this point it levelled off, but then *there was a sudden dip* to below 10 per cent in the month of March.

2 **Write an alternative version of the description in your notebook, changing the verb–adverb phrases in italics to nouns and adjectives and the noun–adjective phrases to verbs and adverbs. Begin with the sentences below.**
In April, the unemployment rate stood at just over 8 per cent. It increased slightly in May but then it remained constant during the month of June.

3 **Circle the correct word to complete the following text.**

STRONG SALES AT IBIS GROUP

Ibis group reported a **1** *successful/successfully* second quarter of trading yesterday with overall sales 3.5 per cent higher than the same period last year. Bonaccord, the flagship fashion outlet, performed very well, with a **2** *steady/steadily* rise in profits from £10.2 million in 2005 to £12.3 million in 2006. The women's clothing department performed very **3** *strong/strongly* and sales were also helped by the **4** *recent/recently* refurbishment of 20 of their stores. Sales also rose **5** *sharp/sharply* at Fragrance, the perfume store which the group acquired in September.

It must be admitted that the figures for Bertrand, the group's fashion outlet for the over-50s, **6** *complete/completely* failed to reflect this success. Here, like-for-like profits fell by 4.1 per cent. However, this poor performance was not **7** *unexpected/unexpectedly* and was partly caused by the wet weather which affected the sales of summer clothes. Mr Tim Wright, chief executive, is **8** *confident/confidently* that things will improve.

Vocabulary

Below you will find two mixed-up descriptions of movements in the share prices of two different companies over a week. Separate the two descriptions by choosing A or B for 1–5 in the box below. Write the two descriptions below.

	A	B
1	The share price rose slightly on Monday and continued …	The share price showed a slight fall on Monday and continued …
2	… to go down the following day. However, …	… to climb the following day. However, …
3	Wednesday saw an end to this downward trend as the price stabilised.	Wednesday saw an end to this upward trend as the price levelled off.
4	There were no further increases on Thursday either but unfortunately on Friday …	There were no further drops in price on Thursday either but on Friday there was a complete change of fortune as …
5	… the price suddenly recovered and rose sharply to exceed even Monday's value.	… the price suddenly plunged to just below Monday's value.

Company X

1 *The share price rose slightly on Monday and continued …*

… to climb the following day. However, …

Company Y

1 *The share price showed a slight fall on Monday and continued …*

… to go down the following day. However, …

UNIT 18 Company finances

Vocabulary

1 Look at this profit and loss account for Sockshow, a company which makes socks. Read the sentences (a–h) and write the correct figures in the profit and loss account.

SOCKSHOW	
Profit and Loss Account	
November	
Sales income	**1** *27,150*
Cost of sales	
Labour	**2** ....
Stock movement	**3** ....
Distribution	**4** ....
Gross profit	19,650
Overheads	
Personnel	**5** ....
Building costs	**6** ....
Stationery and publications	217
Telephone	850
Computer costs	**7** ....
Advertising	1,000
Depreciation*	**8** ....
Total overheads	17,547
Net profit/loss	+2,103

* the reduction in value of an asset over a period of time

In November:

a The total salaries of staff not involved with production (e.g. administrative staff) were £7,540.

b The company used raw materials to the value of £750 to make their products.

c The company spent £840 on new software.

d The company spent £810 on delivering their products.

e The company earned a total of £27,150 from selling the socks.

f The company paid their production staff £5,940 in salaries.

g The estimated fall in value of the company's assets was £1,000.

h They paid £6,100 rent for their office and factory.

2 Complete the following definition.

The net profit or loss is calculated by subtracting the **1** .... from the **2** ....

3 Find 12 finance words in the word square. They can be written across, down or diagonally. Three words are written backwards. The clues below will help you.

r	r	t	d	w	l	o	s	s
e	e	u	e	o	**c**	q	d	s
v	a	r	b	l	**r**	a	e	o
e	n	n	t	f	**e**	s	f	r
n	h	o	o	h	**d**	s	i	g
u	t	v	r	s	**i**	e	c	p
e	n	e	t	a	**t**	t	i	k
f	v	r	m	c	**o**	d	t	p
o	b	a	n	k	**r**	u	p	t

1 Someone who a company must pay money to
2 Someone who owes money to a company (the opposite of **1**)
3 The total sales of a company over a particular period
4 Another word for the money that a company receives over a particular period
5 Rent, electricity bills and administrative costs are all examples of ....
6 The opposite of a profit
7 If a company cannot continue because it is losing money it goes ....
8 The money a company makes *before* deducting the running costs and taxes is the .... profit
9 The money a company makes *after* deducting the running costs and taxes is the .... profit
10 The amount of money that a company has lost
11 The amount of money going into and coming out of a company
12 Something valuable that a company owns, like land or machinery

UNIT 19 Investments

Grammar

1 **Write the effect (1–4) next to the correct cause in the table below.**

1 They are over before investors can take advantage of them
2 They buy more in winter
3 It is difficult to predict
4 People buy less in the summer

Cause	Effect
In December people often feel positive about the New Year	
People are on holiday in July and August	
The stock market is influenced by many different things	
Big gains in share prices usually happen very suddenly	

2 **Complete the following text with the link words in the box. If you have difficulty, look again at page 43 (cause and effect words) and page 52 (contrast words) in the Student's Book. You need to use two words twice.**

so because but however

SEASONAL CHANGES IN SHARE PRICES

There is some evidence that stock markets give better returns at certain times of the year. The traditional idea is that share prices rise in the winter **1** ...*but*... then they fall in the summer. One obvious explanation of this is that people buy less in the summer **2** .... they are on holiday in July and August. In December, people often feel positive about the New Year **3** .... they buy more.

4 .... , most financial advisers do not advise trying to follow seasonal changes in the stock market. The stock market is much more difficult to predict than this **5** .... it is affected by so many different things, like wars and natural disasters. In addition, the really big gains in share prices usually happen very quickly **6** .... they are over before investors can take advantage of them. It is more important to invest for the long term than to try to predict the stock market's every move.

Vocabulary

Complete the crossword below.

Across

6 The collection of shares that someone has (9)
8 A market where share prices are rising is a .... market (4)
9 A company which is at least 51% owned by another is a .... company (10)
10 Part of the money invested in a business (5)
11 The action of making shares available to the public for the first time (9)
12 The result of joining two companies together (6)
13 The part of the company profits which is paid to shareholders (8)

Down

1 Money which is used for investment (7)
2 Profits made from investments (7)
3 A certain quantity of shares (5)
4 Oil, gold and coffee are all examples of .... (11)
5 Someone who can buy and sell shares for you (6)
7 If you don't want to invest in shares, you might invest in these (5)
8 A market where share prices are falling is a .... market (4)

UNIT 20 Starting up

Grammar

1 **Join the sentences using *which*, *who* or *where*. In one of the sentences you need to make a further small change.**

1 Did you read the financial report? It was published yesterday.
Did you read the financial report which was published yesterday?

2 We are writing with regard to invoice number 931. It remains unpaid.

....

3 Yesterday I spoke to your colleague. She told me to phone back today.

....

4 We are staying at a hotel on the Nile. Agatha Christie once stayed there.

....

5 I saw a man on the train. He looked just like your finance director.

....

2 **The following is part of an article about Parker Brothers, a famous American manufacturer of games. Read the account of how they started up and write *who* or *which* in each gap.**

PARKER BROTHERS

Parker Brothers is now a subsidiary of the toy giant Hasbro, but it is still a highly valued brand with a logo which is known throughout the world.

The company started up in the 1880s. George Parker was an enterprising teenager **1** ....*who*.... lived in Salem, Massachusetts. He loved playing different board games with his brothers and friends and formed a special club where they could meet for *this purpose*. Although there were a few board games at that time, most of them were designed to teach moral or religious values. George was not very interested in *these*, so at the age of 16, he invented 'Banking', a game **2** .... was about becoming rich through investments. The members of the club enjoyed it so much that they suggested that George should try to sell it. He offered it to two book publishers **3** .... refused it. Unwilling to give up, George borrowed $50 from his friends and used *this* to produce 500 versions of *the game*. He then went off to sell these around Salem and Boston, the two towns **4** .... he knew best. He returned home with a profit of $100.

This capital was used to set up George S. Parker Company in downtown Salem. George's two brothers soon joined *the enterprise* and it expanded rapidly. By 1888, its catalogue listed 29 games. The most popular games were often those **5** .... were invented by George himself.

3 **Look at the words and expressions in *italics* in the text about the Parker Brothers. Each of them refers to someone or something else in the text. Write what each one refers to.**

1 The company Parker Brothers
2 this purpose ....
3 these ....
4 this ....
5 the game ....
6 This capital ....
7 the enterprise ....

Vocabulary

1 **Circle the correct verb in these sentences.**

1 Your business plan shows that it will be difficult to *cover/wrap/lay* the running costs.
2 The government have *rained/poured/dripped* a lot of money into this project.
3 They *got out/took out/made out* a loan to buy three new company vans.
4 The global vehicle market is preparing for *a/an flood/river/ocean* of new imports from Asia.
5 They had no assets which they could use to *back up/back down/back off* the loan.
6 The bank refused to give us a loan, so it was difficult to *raise/carry/lift* the money to start the business.

2 **We often use verbs to do with travelling and types of transport when describing business ventures or statistics. Complete the following sentences using the verbs and nouns in the box. You will use each one twice, once for a sentence about travelling and once for a sentence about business.**

headed for	took off	ride	~~launch~~	crash

1 A number of celebrities were invited to the launch of our new cruise ship.
2 His career really .... after he completed his business degree.
3 I would love to have a .... in your new Porsche.
4 The secret of a successful product launch is good planning.
5 Share prices fell by over 25 per cent in the stock market .... of 1987.
6 The plane .... from London Heathrow airport at 14.20.
7 In September 1620, the famous ship, the *Mayflower*, left England and .... America.
8 With the current economic uncertainties, I think the stock market is in for a bumpy ....
9 Over fifty people were injured in the train ....
10 Looking at their sales figures, I think the company is .... disaster.

UNIT 21 Job applications

Vocabulary

1 **Look at the table below and change the adjectives to nouns. Two of the most common suffixes for this are *-ness* and *-ity*. Complete the table, being careful to think about any necessary spelling changes. If you need help, look at the sentences in Exercise 2.**

Adjective	Noun
punctual	*punctuality*
polite	
rude	
generous	*generosity*
kind	
sincere	*sincerity*
original	
reliable	
creative	
sensitive	
loyal	

2 **Read the following statements taken from references for job applicants. Decide whether an adjective or a noun is the correct word in each case.**

1 Harriet is an extremely *reliable/reliability* member of staff and has shown *flexible/flexibility* about working extra hours at weekends.

2 Khaled has introduced a number of *original/originality* measures to try to reduce staff costs and his energy and *creative/creativity* have been much appreciated.

3 The department has taken on a number of new members of staff this year and Hiroko has played a key role in helping them. A number of them have commented positively on her *helpful/helpfulness* and *polite/politeness*.

4 Michael has been a *loyal/loyalty* and long-standing member of the company and collegues have often seen him as a source of *stable/stability* in difficult times.

5 Mohan has considerable expertise in managing difficult situations and shows both *sensitive/sensitivity* and skill in dealing with staff.

3 **The phrases in list A are taken from job advertisements and describe the skills that a successful candidate must have. The phrases in list B are taken from the personal profile section of different CVs. Match each skill in list A (1–8) with one in list B (a–h).**

A

1 You need the ability to use your initiative.
2 The successful candidate will have good interpersonal skills.
3 You must be PC literate.
4 You need to show attention to detail.
5 You must show good time-management.
6 You must be committed to lifelong learning.
7 The successful candidate will be able to cope with uncertainty.
8 You must be a good team player.

B

a I have good computer skills.
b I always welcome opportunities for further training and development.
c I work well in a group.
d I am able to organise my work timetable and meet deadlines.
e I am able to work and take decisions independently.
f I am able to complete tasks with precision and accuracy.
g I can form good relationships with many different people.
h I can adapt to changing circumstances and take calculated risks.

Grammar

Complete the following covering letter with the words in the box. There is one word you will not need.

which a where to the ~~in~~ from for also too would

Dear Sir/Madam,

I am writing to express my interest **1** ......*in*...... the position of deputy sales director at Damers, **2** .... is advertised on your website. You will see from my CV that I am **3** .... graduate in business and management **4** .... the University of Sunderland. I have **5** .... recently completed work experience at Carlton and Fisher, **6** .... I was involved in a number of successful projects. I believe that I have **7** .... necessary skills for the post and **8** .... be a strong addition to your management team. I am available **9** .... interview at any time and look forward **10** .... hearing from you.

Yours faithfully,

UNIT 22 Recruitment

Grammar

1 **The text below contains a number of first conditional sentences. Complete the text with the *if* clauses from the box below.**

DISABLED STAFF

1 ......*c*......, most people will think you mean avoiding racial or sexual discrimination. However, there are other types of discrimination too. True diversity means making sure that no group of people is prevented from being a member of your staff because of prejudice.*

Disabled workers are one such group. When we think of a disabled person, we often think of someone with mobility problems who needs to use a wheelchair, but there are other types of disability too, like sight or hearing problems.

Disabled staff have skills and experience which can benefit your business. **2** ...., this will increase the range of candidates for recruiting staff. On the other hand, **3** ...., you may discourage the right person for the job. Not only that, but reports suggest that disabled staff are often very good at creative thinking. This is not surprising, as most of them have to come up with creative solutions to help them in their day-to-day lives. **4** ...., for example, you are likely to be an excellent problem-solver.

The changes needed in the workplace for disabled people are often quite small. You may need to make minor changes to the building and possibly some other changes, depending on the type of disability. For example, **5** ...., company documents may be needed in a different format, like a recording or in large print.

Finally, it is worth remembering that **6** ...., you will probably attract a more diverse range of customers. After all, most disabled people could be your customers as well.

* an unfair or unreasonable feeling against a group of people

a if you are a wheelchair-user who has to travel on the railway
b if you employ someone with sight problems
c ~~if you mention diversity~~
d if disabled people feel they cannot apply
e if you are willing to consider employing a disabled person
f if you have a diverse workforce

2 **Complete the following extracts by putting the verb in brackets in the correct form. Sometimes you will need to form a first and sometimes a second conditional.**

1 My company are cutting a lot of jobs and I think I may well be next on the list. I'm not sure what I *will do* (do) if they *make* (make) me redundant.

2 If I .... (be) you, I .... (not ask) the interviewer about the salary during the interview. I .... (wait) for the job offer first.

3 I don't see any point in having a lot of rules about what you can and can't ask people in interviews. Usually if you .... (not give) people information, they .... (do) everything they can to find out somehow.

4 A: I can't believe my boss spoke to me like that.
B: It really is wrong. I'm lucky because I get on well with my boss but I'm sure if my employer .... (speak) to me like that I .... (start) looking for another job.

5 A: They've offered me the job but I'm not sure if I'll take it.
B: Why not? If someone .... (offer) me a job with a salary like that, I .... (accept) it straight away.

Vocabulary

Complete the following story of how someone lost their job, using the correct word or phrase from the box. You will need one word more than once.

curriculum vitae (CV)	graduate	graduated	human resources	lay off
social networking	redundancy	redundant	turned down	~~unemployed~~

Last week, I was an engineer in a telecommunications company. This week I am **1** *unemployed* !
I heard about the job just after I **2** .... from university. I sent in my **3** .... and, after a short interview, they offered me the position. Ironically, I **4** .... two other job offers later that week.
After just one month, the **5** .... manager called me into her office and told me that the company's sales were much lower than forecast and they had to **6** .... staff. It was 'last in, first out', so I was made **7** .... – I received just one month's **8** .... pay.
I still feel shocked of course, especially as this isn't a very good time for a **9** .... to seek employment. Who knows how long it will take me to find another job? I've updated my **10** .... and have started looking in the newspapers and on the Internet. I've also created a profile on a business networking site as I think **11** .... may be the best way for me to find a job.

UNIT 23 Staff development

Vocabulary

Find 12 words or verbs + preposition associated with human resources in the word square. They can be written horizontally or vertically, but not backwards. Use the clues below to help you.

p	a	m	m	c	w	z	m	l	p	n	y	p
g	p	s	x	r	h	r	e	f	e	r	e	e
s	p	**r**	v	l	f	o	i	f	r	c	e	q
h	r	**é**	j	w	l	i	z	z	s	b	l	o
o	a	**s**	j	t	o	w	k	o	o	p	c	n
r	i	**u**	s	u	g	g	f	t	n	y	n	u
t	s	**m**	q	i	p	y	y	o	n	t	o	a
l	a	**é**	l	a	y	o	f	f	e	d	t	p
i	l	k	c	j	d	t	j	g	l	o	i	v
s	f	l	p	r	o	m	o	t	e	p	c	h
t	w	o	r	k	f	o	r	c	e	b	e	b
d	i	s	m	i	s	s	v	h	b	p	j	o
y	a	u	j	y	x	r	e	t	i	r	e	r
d	q	w	t	u	r	n	d	o	w	n	n	c

1 A US word for 'CV'
2 If you give someone a job in a higher position, you .... them
3 A phrasal verb meaning 'make redundant'
4 The people who work in a company or organisation
5 If people think you are one of the most suitable applicants for a job, you are put on the ....
6 If you remove someone from their job, you .... them
7 The person who gives you a reference
8 If you resign from your job, you hand in your ....
9 A report on an employee which gives details about their performance
10 A phrasal verb, meaning 'reject someone' (for a job)
11 Stop work because of old age
12 Another word for 'staff'

Grammar

The following text is taken from a guide to doing staff appraisals. The words in *italics* are in the wrong form (for example a verb is written instead of a noun or an adjective instead of an adverb). Read the text and change the words in *italics* to the correct form.

Staff appraisals are very important. They can make the difference between a committed, successful team and a personnel disaster. However, they can also be tricky to get right. Here are some basic guidelines.

- Set a time and date for the appraisal and stick to it.
- Appraisals are an opportunity to discuss the employee's **1** ~~*perform*~~ *performance* so don't be tempted to start discussing other issues.
- Try to get an objective view of the employee's **2** *perform* by asking other members of the **3** *manage* team for their opinions too.
- Don't take calls or allow **4** *interrupt* during the appraisal. This shows that you take the procedure **5** *serious.*
- Listen to the employee. Don't talk too much yourself, even if you think that your superior **6** *know* can solve the employee's problems.
- Don't only give **7** *criticise.* If the appraisal is too negative, the employee may become **8** *demotivation.*
- Appraisals can also be too positive, so that the employee thinks 'I am so good, there is nothing I need to **9** *improvement'.* You can **10** *avoidance* both of these traps by using the company standards and the job description to **11** *measurement* how well the employee is doing.
- Write up the results **12** *prompt.*

UNIT 24 Employee productivity

Grammar

Complete the text by putting the verbs in brackets in the infinitive or *-ing* form.

DEADLINES

Relatively few people are able **1** *to motivate* (motivate) themselves without deadlines. However, **2** .... (set) effective deadlines is a challenge. If they are too easy, this will encourage people **3** .... (waste) time. On the other hand, if they are too challenging or impossible **4** .... (achieve), this will cause staff **5** .... (become) demotivated, because if people think they simply cannot do something in the given time, they will stop **6** .... (try).

People always put off **7** .... (work) on things when the deadline is far in the future. For example, if it is necessary **8** .... (complete) a project in a month's time, you need **9** .... (break) down this deadline into a number of smaller, more immediate ones. If you give people deadlines which relate to small chunks of work that they are capable of **10** .... (achieve) in one or two days, then they are more likely **11** .... (work) efficiently. It is also a good idea **12** .... (make) the deadlines public, or at least **13** .... (write) them down. **14** .... (put) a deadline on paper always makes it more powerful.

Vocabulary

Some compound nouns refer to *types* of people. Complete the statements below, using the correct type of person from the box. Try to do this without using a dictionary. Instead, look at the individual words which form the compound nouns.

high flier	perfectionist	problem solver	star performer	team player	~~workaholic~~

1 He finds it difficult to stop thinking about work and he's often in the office at weekends. He's such a *workaholic* .

2 I'm sure he'll move into a top position very soon because he's so ambitious. He's a real ....

3 She's never satisfied until a piece of work is as good as she can make it. She's a ....

4 He's definitely the best executive we've ever had and our market share has really improved under him. He's our ....

5 She's very good at working with other people and reducing conflict between them. She's a good ....

6 He's very good at creative thinking and finding ways out of difficulties. He's a great ....

Grammar and vocabulary

Complete the following short article. Choose the correct word A, B or C to fill each gap (1–16).

INTERRUPTIONS

One of the biggest threats to employee productivity is the interruption. In order **1** ......A...... work effectively, people need long periods of uninterrupted time, **2** .... that they can really concentrate **3** .... the task that they have to do. This is especially true of creative people **4** .... need time to think about their ideas and explore **5** .... fully.

Some people blame new methods of communication like emails or text messages for **6** .... a constant source of interruption, **7** .... at least you can choose when to respond to these. You can **8** .... off your mobile and you can leave your email until the end of the day. There are very **9** .... emails that **10** .... to be answered immediately. No, the real problems are the meetings, the phone calls and the interruptions from colleagues and managers.

So what can be done? Some companies **11** .... created a no-email day when nobody is allowed to email anyone **12** ...., but as we have seen, emails are not really the problem. Jason Fried, the founder of the software company 37Signals, has **13** .... up with a different idea. He suggests creating a no-talk day, perhaps just once **14** .... month at first, when employees have to work in silence. It sounds strange, but **15** .... my opinion, it might well be worth trying. Who knows, it might **16** .... out to be the most productive day of the month!

1	A to	B for	C of
2	A so	B but	C and
3	A at	B in	C on
4	A which	B who	C what
5	A it	B they	C them
6	A be	B are	C being
7	A so	B but	C and
8	A turn	B lay	C put
9	A few	B little	C several
10	A must	B need	C should
11	A have	B are	C has
12	A also	B else	C other
13	A put	B made	C come
14	A a	B the	C some
15	A in	B of	C at
16	A come	B turn	C find

Writing supplement

Punctuation

Capitalisation

1 **Below you will find a list of rules of when you need to use capital letters in English. Match (1–10) with the correct example (a–j).**

1 names of countries ....*c*.......
2 nationality adjectives and languages ....
3 cities and place names ....
4 nouns when they are part of place names ....
5 companies and institutions ....
6 many abbreviations ....
7 names of books, newspapers, etc. ....
8 titles when they are part of people's names ....
9 days of the week ....
10 months of the year ....

a June, November
b *Financial Times, Business Benchmark*
c Italy, China
d CEO, GDP
e Samsung, Harvard Business School
f Dr Johnson, President Kennedy
g Italian, Chinese
h Sunday, Thursday
i Wall Street, the City of London
j Bangkok, the Nile

2 **Insert capital letters into the following email in the correct places. You will need to put them at the beginning of the sentences as well.**

hi mark,

just thought i'd drop you a quick email from brussels. the visit to hedex seems to be going well. my french isn't that good as you know but most of the directors here speak really good english. hopefully, i'll come back with a definite order.

my hotel is really nice, quite near to grand place, which is very central. i don't think i'll have time for much sightseeing but i saw the nato headquarters from the taxi yesterday.

i'm catching the eurostar back to london on thursday so i'll give you a call that evening. hopefully, we can meet up some weekend later in april.

speak soon,

rosemary

Apostrophes

1 Match the rules for using apostrophes with the correct examples (a–f).

1 We use apostrophes where letters are missing in contractions. ...b...
2 We use apostrophes to indicate possessive *s*. If the noun is singular, the apostrophe comes before the *s*. ....
3 To indicate the possessive with plural nouns, we put an apostrophe after the *s*. We do not usually add *'s*. ....
4 If the plural does not finish in *s* we add an apostrophe and an *s* (just as for singular nouns). ....
5 Possessive pronouns do not use apostrophes. ....
6 In the case of companies named after the founder, some choose to use an apostrophe and some don't. ....

a children's toys, women's fashion items
b it's, haven't, shouldn't
c the trainees' uniforms, the candidates' CVs
d yours, its, theirs
e the director's wife, Paul's office
f Barclays Bank, Harrods, McDonald's, Sainsbury's

2 Add apostrophes where necessary to the following sentences.

1 James – I *can't* find *David's* telephone number – please can you send it to me?
2 We are one of Europes largest holiday companies.
3 Browse our unique range of ladies watches from our online store.
4 Mens shoes upstairs.
5 Your companys contact details will be included on our members page.
6 Credit Suisse saw its share price fall by 4.5 per cent.

Full stops and commas

1 Match the rules (1–6) for using commas with the example sentences (a–f) on the next page.

1 Commas are used between items in a list, except when there is 'and' before the item. ...e...
2 Link words which join two ideas in one sentence, like 'but' and 'so', can have a comma before them. ....
3 When the link word moves to the beginning of the sentence, the two sentence halves are separated by a comma. ....
4 Adverbs at the beginning of a sentence, and link words like 'however', usually have a comma after them. ....
5 When 'that' is used in a relative clause, it doesn't have a comma before it. ....
6 The openings of formal letters like 'Dear Sir' usually have a comma after them. ....

a I would like some information about the courses that you run.
b Although the location is good, the rent is too high for our budget.
c We do not usually give discounts above 5 per cent, but we are willing to make an exception in this case.
d Unfortunately, I will be out of the office on 9 February. However, my deputy, Ian Roper, will be pleased to show you around.
e Our desserts come in three flavours: chocolate, strawberry and vanilla.
f Dear Sir,
I am writing to apply for the position of marketing executive ...

2 It is not usually good style to link phrases in English with commas, although you may see it in some informal writing. You should usually start a new sentence or add a link word instead. Replace the commas in the following emails with the most suitable link word.

1

> Hi Franco
> Just a note to say thanks so much for taking the materials to the Unifreight office last night. I know it was a long day for you, you wanted to get home, I really appreciate it.

2

> Hi Jenny
> I think your design for the flyers is great, we can't change them now, they have already gone to the printers. I will keep your design on file, maybe we can use it for the next batch.

3 Write out the following memo with the correct punctuation. You will need to insert full stops, apostrophes, commas and capital letters.

> the purpose of this memo is to record two conversations with amanda todd regarding her use of the office phone
>
> i first raised the issue with amanda on 14 may amanda explained that she lived with her elderly mother who was in poor health she said that she needed to check up on her during the day i pointed out that she could use her mobile for this and that employees use of the phone should be limited to work-related issues however the bill that I received after this conversation showed no reduction in the number of amandas phone calls
>
> in a meeting on 12 june amanda said again that the calls were to her mother she said that she could not use her mobile for this because the signal was not always clear i told her that although we sympathise with her situation we cannot accept this number of personal calls as well as the cost they take up too much of her work time i also told her that if she does not reduce the number and length of these calls we will have to issue her with a written warning

Spelling

1 *-er / -or*

It can be difficult to know if the name of a job or role ends in *-er* or *-or*. Most nouns which come directly from verbs, like *cleaner*, use *-er*. Many professional titles and roles use *-or* but there are a number of exceptions. Complete the following words with *-er* or *-or*.

1 invest...*or*...	2 distribut............
3 interview............	4 audit............
5 suppli............	6 lawy............
7 consum............	8 sharehold............
9 plumb............	10 edit............
11 credit............	12 visit............

2 *-c / -k / -ck*

***-ck* is used at the end of a word after a single vowel. *-k* is used after a consonant or two vowels. English words do not often end in *-c*. The exception is the *-ic* suffix found at the end of many adjectives, e.g. *fantastic*.**

Correct the spelling mistakes in the following compound nouns and collocations. If there is no mistake, write *correct*.

1 a trak record ...*track*...
2 a block booking ....
3 gross domestick product ....
4 a peack period ....
5 the stock market ....
6 a classic example ....
7 a blanck cheque ....
8 publicity seecking ....

3 *ie / ei*

People often learn the expression 'i before e except after c'. Compare, for example, the spellings of *field* and *ceiling*. However, the rule only works when the letters are pronounced /iː/. With other pronunciations, *ei* can be used after any letter, e.g. *weight*.

Complete the following words with *-ie* or *–ei*.

1 bel...*ie*...ve	2 br............f
3 rec............ve	4 gr............vance
5 fr............ght	6 ach............ve
7 h............ght	8 n............ghbour
9 dec............ve	10 rec............pt

4 **Doubling consonants**

Double consonants are often used to show that the vowel before them has a short sound and not a long sound. For example, compare the pronunciations of *later* and *matter*. This means that you sometimes need to double the final consonant of a word if you add a suffix. Consonants are doubled when they come after a single vowel and only on stressed syllables. See page 19 of the Student's Book for details.

Underline the correct spellings in the two alternatives.

1 begining / beginning
2 droped / dropped
3 heating / heatting
4 contained / containned
5 happened / happenned
6 auditing / auditting
7 commited/ committed
8 targeted / targetted
9 profitable / profittable
10 equiped / equipped
11 reference / referrence
12 transfered / transferred

5 **Suffixes and words that end in *e***

When you add a suffix which begins with a vowel, e.g. *-ing* or *-ous*, to a word ending in *e*, drop the final *e*, e.g. *fame – famous*. When you add a suffix which begins with a consonant, e.g. *-ment* or *-ly*, keep the final *e*, e.g. *improve – improvement*. In certain cases, the rule is broken to keep the original sound of a *c* or *g* before the final *e*, e.g. *noticeable*.

Add the suffixes in brackets to the following words. In some cases, you must drop the final *e* and in some you must keep it.

1 retire (ment) ...*retirement*...
2 package (ing) ....
3 arrange (ment) ....
4 close (ly) ....
5 insure (ance) ....
6 machine (ist) ....
7 bore (dom) ....
8 generate (ive) ....
9 unfortunate (ly) ....
10 consume (ables) ....
11 safe (ty) ....
12 advise (able) ....

6 **Silent consonants**
Some English words contain silent consonants. This is usually for historical reasons. Find 12 words with a silent consonant in the following word square.

F	E	**F**	**A**	**S**	**T**	**E**	**N**	D	A
K	N	O	W	L	E	D	G	E	H
C	A	M	P	A	I	G	N	B	O
S	K	H	O	N	E	S	T	T	U
Q	G	M	X	Q	B	Z	O	Y	R
W	H	R	E	S	I	G	N	D	C
R	U	C	O	L	U	M	N	C	K
A	H	D	A	K	B	O	M	B	H
P	S	Y	C	H	O	L	O	G	Y
O	C	R	E	C	E	I	P	T	W

7 **Find and correct ten spelling mistakes in the following emails.**

Dear Mr Anderson,
I am writing with ~~referrence~~ *reference* to order 2547 which we recieved on 12 May. Although all the items were correctly listed on the invoice, unfortunatly, the cutlery that we ordered was missing. Instead of cutlery, one of the crates containned a duplicate set of glassware. Please could you make arrangments to deliver the missing cutlery as soon as possible and let us know how we should return the second set of glassware.
Yours sincerly,
Hideko Miyoshi

Dear Ms Miyoshi,
We are sorry about the mistake in your order, which evidently happenned at the packing stage. We have now dispatched the missing cutlery and we will arrange for one of our distributers to pik up the extra glassware within the next two weeks. We would be grateful if you could leave it in the original packageing. Once again, please accept our apologies for the inconvenience.
Kind regards,
Thomas Anderson

Writing fluently

Pronouns and reference words

1 **You need to use pronouns in your own writing to avoid too much repetition. You practised identifying what the pronouns in a text referred to in Unit 18 (page 89) and Grammar workshop 5 (page 98) of the Student's Book. Complete the following sentences with the most suitable pronoun from the box. There are more pronouns than you need.**

he him ~~it~~ they them one this these

1. We enjoyed your course very much and found ....*it*.... very useful.
2. Thank you for sending me the feedback results. I would like to discuss .... in our next meeting.
3. I have received the sales figures that you sent me but .... do not seem to be complete.
4. Mr Rose is one of our most important clients. I would like you to meet .... as soon as possible.
5. It seems clear that you posted confidential company information on your blog. We regard .... as very serious misconduct.
6. I have a copy of last year's price list but I really need a more up to date ....

2 **We can also use *this* + a general noun to avoid repeating something we have already talked about. Complete the following sentences, using the general nouns in the box.**

event service ~~figure~~ matter policy date

1. Your report gives the total sales as 2405 units but this ....*figure*.... is incorrect.
2. Thank you for your email regarding free valuations. However, I am afraid we no longer offer this ....
3. The deadline for applications is 30 March. Applications received after this .... will not be considered.
4. The company does not permit job-sharing and I am afraid we have no plans to change this ....
5. I am interested in attending the trade fair and would be grateful if you could send me some further information about this ....
6. I am writing with regard to my insurance claim for fire damage. I have already contacted you twice about this ....

3 Read the following letter from the finance department of a company to a customer. At the moment this letter is too repetitive. Write an improved version in your notebook by replacing the underlined words and phrases with the reference words and phrases in the box below.

> Dear Mr Wells,
> I am writing with regard to payment for invoice 2581. According to our records we have still not received payment for invoice 2581. I emailed you about the fact that we have not received payment for invoice 2581 on 8 November and I also spoke to a member of your finance team the following week.
> I would be grateful if you could make payment for invoice 2581 as soon as possible and by 10 December at the latest. If we do not receive payment for invoice 2581 by 10 December, we will be unable to supply you with further goods.
> I enclose a copy of invoice 2581 for your reference.

it	this	this payment	the relevant invoice	this matter	this date

Link words: contrasts

1 Link words make your writing better because they tell your reader how the ideas are related. One common relationship is contrast. You practised the language for making contrasts in Unit 10 (page 52) and Grammar workshop 3 (page 62) of the Student's Book. Read the following sentences and match each one with the correct source (a–e).

1. Spending on toys is predicted to remain high despite the economic downturn. ....b....
2. Although your qualifications are clearly relevant, we decided to appoint a candidate with more previous experience. ....
3. Whereas most ready meals contain artificial preservatives, our new range contains nothing but fresh, natural ingredients. ....
4. We are not legally obliged to offer a refund, but will offer a £50 credit note as a goodwill gesture. ....
5. My order was for 100 medium size and 100 large T-shirts. However, when I opened the crate I found that they were all medium size. ....

a an email to a supplier
b an article from the financial news
c an advertisement for new products
d a letter to a dissatisfied customer
e a letter to an unsuccessful applicant for a job

2 Underline the contrast word in the sentences in Exercise 1. Then complete the following rules with the correct contrast words from the box.

but ~~however~~ despite although

1 ......*however*...... contrasts two separate sentences and is followed by a comma.
2 .... usually contrasts two ideas in one sentence and must be placed in the middle of the sentence.
3 .... contrasts two ideas in one sentence and can be placed at the beginning of the sentence. In this case we need to put a comma in the middle.
4 .... also contrasts two ideas in one sentence and can be placed at the beginning.

3 *Whereas* is a link word which we often use to compare two things. Which of the four rules above does it follow?

4 Unscramble phrases (1–4) and then insert them in the correct places (A–D) in the following letters. Add commas if necessary.
1 miss will certainly although here I working
2 telephone numerous despite calls
3 three later not did the arrive goods however weeks until
4 hope but colleagues here stay contact to with in I

Dear Mr Sinclair,
I am writing with regard to order 3546 which was placed on 21 July.
I was told to expect delivery after one week. **A** *However, the goods did not arrive until three weeks later* and then a number of items were missing.
B .... I have still not received these items and your staff have been unable to give me a further delivery date.
I am most disappointed at your company's poor customer service and will not be placing any further orders with you.
Yours,
Barbara Boschi

Dear Mr Walton,
I am writing to confirm that I wish to resign my current position at Letchford's.
As you know, I have been offered a senior position with Foster and Burke in Manchester. **C** .... I do not feel I can turn down this opportunity.
Moving to Manchester is of course a big step **D** .... In the meantime, I would like to thank you for your support over the past four years.
Yours sincerely,
Simon Lewis

Link words: causes, effects and purposes

1 Link words can also show cause and effect. You practised the language for this in Unit 8 (pages 42 and 43) and Grammar workshop 2 (page 45) of the Student's Book. Read the following extracts and write whether each clause is a cause (C) or an effect (E) of an action.

1 Please could staff note that the parking area to the right of the office building will be closed for the next month ..*E*.... <u>because</u> building work is taking place ..*C*.... .

2 The seminar room is currently being used to store furniture .... <u>so</u> the training session today will take place in room 7 ....

3 Please note that Abdul Rahmani from the accounts department will be on leave for the next two weeks .... <u>This means that</u> you will need to send any expenses claims to Jane Foley instead ....

4 The security cameras on the shop floor will be updated next week .... <u>This is because</u> there have been a number of cases of theft recently ....

2 Which of the underlined phrases:

1 are followed by a cause of the previous action? ..*because*........ , ...

2 are followed by an effect of the previous action? .... , ...

3 join the ideas in one sentence? .... , ...

4 are used to start a new sentence? .... , ...

3 Read the following memos which both give instructions and the purposes for them. Which of the underlined phrases is followed by:

- an infinitive?
- a phrase with a modal verb?

1

<u>In order to</u> reduce our electricity bills, please could staff make sure that all electrical appliances they have used are completely switched off before they leave the building?

2

Please could all staff fill in the information on the attached form <u>so that</u> we can update our staff records?

4 Complete the following notes and memos with the most suitable phrase from the box and add a suitable link word or phrase.

a number of accounts have been hacked	make office communications clearer
I can contact you if there are any delays	~~please cd you call back asap?~~
we want to make a good impression on our visitors	

1

John phoned while you were away. Said it was quite urgent *so please cd you call back asap?*

2 ...., please could staff follow the attached guidelines when writing all staff emails and memos.

3 Looking forward to seeing you again tomorrow. Can you text me your mobile number just .... ? Thanks.

4 All staff are advised to change their computer passwords immediately. ....

5 Please could all staff spend a few minutes tidying their desks before they leave this evening ....

Link words: addition

1 **Read the following advertisement and answer the questions about the addition link words.**

> **HALES CAR HIRE**
>
> Hales are your top choice if you need to hire a car. We also hire out commercial vans for businesses.
>
> The period of hire is flexible and vehicle availability is guaranteed if you book in advance. If you need multiple vehicles, we can also put together a hire package to meet your requirements.
>
> We offer a range of different insurance options as well as £10 worth of petrol with every hire.

1 Which link word/phrase joins two clauses in one sentence? *and*
2 Which link word/phrase goes in a new sentence? ....
3 Which link word/phrase is usually followed by a noun? ....
4 *Also* should not usually be put at the beginning of the sentence. Complete the rules by circling the correct alternative:
   a *Also* is placed before/after the main verb in the sentence.
   b When there is an auxiliary verb or modal verb in a sentence, *also* is placed before/after it.

2 **Complete the following advertisement by writing *and*, *also* or *as well as* in each gap.**

> **PEPPERS CATERING**
>
> Peppers offers catering services for weddings, celebrations **1** *and* corporate events. A wide choice of menus is available.
> We prepare the food on our premises **2** .... deliver it in our refrigerated vans. We can **3** .... prepare the dishes on your premises. **4** .... the food, our menu price package includes all table linen, crockery **5** .... cutlery.

3 Complete the following emails. Choose the correct link word or phrase (A, B or C) to fill each gap.

Dear all,

We have just heard that there will be a transport strike tomorrow. **1** ...B... there will be very few buses **2** .... the trains are likely to be very crowded during the rush hour. **3** .... any members of staff wish to come in later or work from home, this may be possible, **4** .... please let me know by the end of today.

Rosaria

1 A This is because	B This means that	C However
2 A and	B but	C because
3 A When	B If	C Because
4 A however	B despite	C but

Dear Mr Davies,

Many thanks for your email giving the details of your visit next month. We have booked you three nights in the Hotel Tamanaco. **5** .... this is further from us than the hotel we usually use, it is very comfortable **6** .... taxis are relatively cheap here.

We are currently putting together a programme for the visit **7** .... please could you let us know if there is anything you would especially like to see? I would also be grateful if you could confirm your flight details as soon as possible **8** .... we can arrange a meet-and-greet at the airport.

We look forward to meeting you.

Kind regards,

Silvana San Vicente

5 A But	B Despite	C Although
6 A but	B and	C so
7 A so	B because	C also
8 A in order to	B so that	C because

To all staff:

Please note that we will be upgrading the system tomorrow. **9** .... email will not be accessible, **10** .... you will still be able to create and print documents. We hope to have everything up and running by the afternoon. **11** .... , it's probably best not to rely on this **12** .... there may be a few unexpected problems.

IT department

9 A This is because	B This means that	C However
10 A so	B because	C although
11 A Despite	B Whereas	C However
12 A because	B so	C but

Organising your writing

Beginnings and endings

1 **Emails and letters often start and end with particular types of sentences. Decide if the following are likely to appear at the beginning (B) or end (E) of an email.**

1 a hope or wish for the future ...E...
2 the main reason for writing ....
3 a reference to possible enquiries or communications in the future ....
4 information about who the writer is or where s/he is from ....
5 a reference to a previous email or communication ....
6 a reminder of the main reason why the email was written ....

2 **Match (1–6) in Exercise 1 with one of the sentences below (a–f).**

a I am writing on behalf of Guilden Business College.
b Once again, many congratulations on winning this award.
c I look forward to meeting you again at future conferences. *1*
d If you have any further questions, please do not hesitate to contact me.
e I am writing to complain about the actions of one of your sales staff.
f Thank you for your letter of 25 July.

Giving additional information

1 **The main part of an email or letter will give the reason for writing and add other details too. Match the following sentences (1–4) with the information or question that follows it (a–d).**

1 I would be grateful if you could send a list of available dates for your training workshops. ...d...
2 We will be happy to accept payment in three instalments, as you propose. ....
3 Please could you bring a document which confirms your name and address. ....
4 I am pleased to inform you that your bid for the Arcadia Bridge engineering project was successful. ....

a May I say we were particularly impressed by your proposal for online project updates.
b However, the total balance must be cleared by the end of July.
c This is because we are required by law to check your identity.
d Please could you also let me know if you can run them onsite?

2 **Which continuation:**

1 makes an additional enquiry or request? ...d...
2 gives a specific detail? ....
3 gives a condition to what is agreed? ....
4 gives a reason for a request? ....

3 **Below you will find two mixed up emails (A and B). Write the two emails in the correct order in your notebook.**

> I would also like to know if you can arrange delivery.
> We will also carry out a full check of the whole system.
> Please could you let me know if you have anything suitable in stock?
> I am sorry to hear of the problems you have experienced with the new security system.
> *B* I am writing with regard to your website which advertises second-hand office furniture.
> We have arranged for our maintenance team to visit your office on 20 September to locate the error.
> I am currently looking for five large filing cabinets.
> I can be contacted on this email or on 07869 456734.
> *A* Re: your letter of 15 September.
> Once again, please accept our apologies.

Paragraphing

1 **Formal letters and longer emails need to be divided into paragraphs. Look at the following letter of application. There are three paragraphs. Which paragraph:**

1 refers to future communications with Mr Anderson? ....*c*....
2 gives reasons why Ms Woodin is a suitable person for the job? ....
3 gives the main reason for writing? ....

> Dear Mr Anderson,
>
> a I would like to apply for the post of personal assistant as advertised on your website.
>
> b You will see from the attached CV that I already have five years' experience of working in a similar capacity at Fisons. My job there involved dealing with office communications and correspondence on a daily basis. I am a competent user of most computer software packages and have some knowledge of accounting systems. I believe I have the necessary skills for the post.
>
> c I am available for interview at your earliest convenience. I look forward to hearing from you.
>
> Yours sincerely,
>
> Bethany Woodin

2 **Decide if the following statements about paragraphs are true or false. Use the letter above to help you. Write T or F.**

1 When you look at a letter or text, you can see how many paragraphs there are. ....*T*....
2 Each paragraph deals with a different aspect of what you are writing about. ....

3 You should leave a line space between paragraphs. ....
4 The first line of a new paragraph always starts about 3 cm away from the margin. ....
5 You start each new sentence on a new line in a paragraph. ....
6 A paragraph always contains more than one sentence. ....

3 **Read the following company profile from the home page of a website. Divide it into four paragraphs.**

When Paolo Perri moved to London from Naples over ten years ago, there was one thing he missed. That was real Italian ice cream. He couldn't find it in any of the local stores, so he decided to set up his own company. That was the beginning of Gelateria Perri. Now we have grown from one single London shop to a company with over fifteen outlets. We have just opened our first outlet outside London, in the seaside town of Brighton. Not only that, but we supply our products nationwide to a number of key players in the hospitality industry. Our ice cream is always made from fresh ingredients and contains no artificial flavourings. You will find our eight key flavours in any of our stores but we can also create flavours on request. As well as ice cream, we now produce a number of other popular frozen desserts. To contact us, log on to sales@gelateriaperri.co.uk. Alternatively, drop into any of our ice cream stores. We are always willing to discuss your business needs and we take pride in our personal customer service.

4 **Give each paragraph a title. Try to use no more than three words for each one.**

5 **Read the following letter and decide where the paragraphs should begin and end. There should be four paragraphs in total.**

Dear Sirs,
We at the Young Entrepreneurs Society are planning to hold an exhibition this summer and we are writing to ask if your company would be willing to sponsor a stand at this event. The exhibition will be held on 25 July at the Park Hotel. It will provide an opportunity for our most promising young business people to present their services and products and, as a sponsor, your company would benefit from all the publicity for the event. We expect several thousand people to attend, including a number of well-known personalities from the business world. There will also be a programme of entertainment. We have several different packages for sponsorship. Please find details on the sponsorship forms enclosed with this letter. We also enclose a brochure giving further information about our society and the work that we do. We look forward to hearing from you and thank you in advance.
Yours faithfully,
Pat Samuda

6 **Put the following sentences in order to create a reply to the above letter. Then write the letter out in your notebook, dividing it into three paragraphs.**

Dear Ms Samuda, Unfortunately, I am afraid we are unable to sponsor the event at this time. Your society clearly does very valuable work in encouraging and supporting young business people. Thank you for your letter giving details about the Young Entrepreneurs exhibition on 25 July. Please accept our best wishes for the success of the event. Although our internal budget does not allow us to provide funding, a member of our management team would be delighted to attend the exhibition. Yours sincerely, Donald Kantor

Answer key

Unit 1

Vocabulary

1 **Personnel:** staff, recruitment, workforce, human resources
Accounts: payroll, salary, bookkeeping, expenditure
Sales: retail outlet, consumer, mail order, wholesale

3 2 look up 3 book 4 lead 5 install 6 work on 7 pay 8 recruit

Grammar

1 2 read 3 wants 4 are/'re reviewing 5 check 6 have 7 seems, are not/ aren't buying 8 are/'re thinking, need

2 *Suggested answers*
2 What do people like on Marie Riley's show?
3 Is David Webb worried by the figures?
4 Who is Radio Heartbeat trying to appeal to?
5 Why is David Webb sure that Johnny can bring listeners in? / Why does David Webb have confidence in Johnny?
6 What is Morgan Wells thinking of doing?

Unit 2

Reading

2 d 3 b 4 a 5 g 6 i 7 f 8 e

Vocabulary

2 copy 3 download 4 attach 5 hack 6 forward 7 surf 8 reboot

Grammar and vocabulary

2 A 3 C 4 B 5 B 6 A 7 A 8 B 9 B 10 C

Unit 3

Grammar 1

2 2 ran 3 did not/didn't make 4 limited 5 did not/didn't operate 6 grew

3 *Suggested answers*
2 What did the company manufacture at first?
3 Where did Azim Premji study?
4 When did Azim Premji take over the company? / When did Mr M.H. Premji die?
5 In the 70s and 80s, why did many multinational companies stop trading in India/leave India?
6 When did Azim Premji set up the first IT business in Bangalore?

Grammar 2

1 2 met, was studying
3 was waiting, came
4 looked, saw
5 broke, was having
6 told, was raining
7 left, breathed
8 were/was planning, offered

2 2 was feeding 3 noticed 4 gave 5 produced 6 set

Unit 4

Reading

after-work activities	5
working hours	4
equal opportunities	2

Vocabulary

1 *Suggested answers*
verb–noun: take responsibility, commission a report, encourage movement, provide support
adjective–noun: strong commitment, professional qualifications, flexible working, intensive work, keen sportsperson

2 2 bring up
3 grow
4 found
5 transport

3 2 transfer
3 open
4 take out
5 charge
6 pay off

4 1 individual needs
2 diverse workforce, global market
3 profitable solutions, innovative technology
4 wide range, high standard

Unit 5

Vocabulary

1

Noun	Adjective
a circle	circular
an oval	oval
a triangle	triangular
a square	square
a sphere	spherical
a cylinder	cylindrical
a cone	conical

2 a V-shaped
b pear-shaped
c star-shaped
d mushroom-shaped

3 2 a 3 h 4 e 5 f 6 c 7 d 8 g

4 2 d 3 a 4 c 5 f 6 b

5 2 A 3 B 4 B 5 B 6 A

6 2 The toner in the photocopier needs changing.
3 The photocopier keeps overheating.
4 The computer keyboard needs cleaning.
5 The buttons on the machine keep jamming.

Unit 6

Grammar 1

2 The bathrooms are inspected every three hours.
3 Previous invoices are kept in the filing cabinet.
4 The staff are paid on the last working day of the month.
5 Discounts are given for all orders over £300.
6 All the bags are checked by the security guard.
7 Gloves are worn when the staff mix the oil.
8 The perfume bottles are packed into boxes by machines.
9 Cold air is blown over the mixture to cool it.

Vocabulary

2 dissolves 3 evaporates 4 distil
5 extract

Grammar 2

2 2 is distilled 3 is used
4 does not/doesn't go 5 are dried
6 are used 7 includes 8 are sold
9 are exported 10 employ
11 are taken on 12 remains 13 work

Unit 7

Grammar

2 should not 3 don't have to 4 must not
5 can, should not

Vocabulary

1 2 d 3 f 4 g 5 a 6 e 7 h 8 b

2 2 get through 3 put you on hold
4 put me through
5 are/'re breaking up 6 cut off

3 *Suggested answer*
A: Baron Electronics. How can I help?
B: I'd like to speak to Mr Rosen, please.
A: He's not here at the moment. Can I take a message?
B: Yes. Please could you ask him to phone me as soon as possible?
A: Can I ask who's calling, please?
B: Yes. It's Mr Reinhardt from the Cooperative Bank.
A: How do you spell your name?
B: R-E-I-N-H-A-R-D-T.

Grammar and vocabulary

2 B 3 C 4 A 5 B 6 A 7 C 8 B
9 C 10 B

Unit 8

Vocabulary

Across: 3 sample 5 campaign 6 agency 8 logo 9 word of mouth 10 market share
Down: 1 slogan 2 flyer 3 sponsor 4 market leader 7 competitor 11 ad

Grammar

1 2 a 3 e 4 d 5 f 6 b
2 2 because many people are annoyed by uninvited phone calls.
3 so it is important to carry out market research.
4 so companies have to continually develop new ones.
5 so they often continue to buy a particular one.
6 because people tell their friends about both good and bad experiences.
3 2 in order to 3 in order to 4 so 5 Because 6 so

Unit 9

Grammar 1

2 am/'m flying 3 am/'m coming 4 am/'m staying 5 are you going to do 6 am/'m going to check 7 will fall

Grammar 2

2 the 3 to 4 them 5 its 6 with 7 for 8 in 9 up 10 and 11 this 12 can 13 when 14 about 15 still 16 a

Vocabulary

2 free 3 booked up 4 do 5 suit 6 work

Unit 10

Vocabulary 1

1 **Road:** bypass, lorry, traffic jam
Rail: track, platform
Air: runway, stopover, take-off
All three: signal, delay, crash, freight
2 2 aisle seat 3 flight attendant, board/get on the plane 4 swap seats 5 emergency exit, overhead locker 6 get off the plane/land

Grammar

1 2 Although 3 However 4 Despite
2 *Suggested answer*
High speed railways are a big business in China and have attracted a great deal of investment. The system started in 2007 with less than 250,000 passengers a day but now the number has reached over 800,000. You can now travel from Beijing to Shanghai in about five hours, whereas only a few years ago it took twice as long. However, this rapid growth has also seen some setbacks, like the serious train crash in Wenzhou in July 2011. Despite this, safety standards on Chinese railways remain high.

Vocabulary 2

Suggested answers
2 boring 3 doing well/growing 4 difficult 5 fall/drop

Unit 11

Grammar

1 2 longer 3 lower 4 better 5 fitter 6 higher 7 more important 8 less/more demanding
2 2 as bad as
3 as early as
4 as long as
5 as simple/easy as

Grammar and vocabulary

2 C 3 B 4 C 5 B 6 A 7 B 8 C 9 B 10 A 11 C 12 A

Unit 12

Grammar

Suggested answers
3 more helpful 4 larger 5 the dullest 6 longer 7 the most useful 8 more entertaining

Vocabulary

1 *Suggested answers*
wear a badge; give a lecture/a presentation; put up signs; attend a presentation/a lecture; book the venue; give out a feedback form/information packs; fill in a feedback form

2 **A delegate:** attend a lecture/a presentation; fill in a feedback form; wear a badge
A speaker: give a presentation/lecture; wear a badge
An organiser: book the venue; give out information packs/a feedback form; put up signs; wear a badge

Unit 13

Grammar

1 2 chose 3 earned 4 became 5 has been 6 has expanded 7 has become 8 has established 9 passed 10 has always insisted 11 have called 12 have made

2
2 We have/'ve had the new machinery since January.
3 I have/'ve known your CEO for several years.
4 He has/'s lived in California since 2009/for X years.
5 Mr Boston has/'s been on holiday for five days.
6 I have/'ve done/been doing this job since 2008/ for X years.
7 We have/'ve used that supplier for ages.
8 James has not/hasn't worked in/for this company since April.

Vocabulary

2 vary 3 convert 4 move 5 revolutionise 6 adapt 7 revise 8 swap

Unit 14

Grammar

1
2 *Correct*
3 *Correct*
4 ~~These furnitures are~~ **This furniture is** not very suitable for our office.
5 I'm afraid ~~progresses~~ **progress** with this project ~~have~~ **has** been rather slow.
6 *Correct*
7 All the ~~evidences suggest~~ **evidence suggests** that tax cuts can encourage economic growth.
8 He crashed the car this morning but fortunately the ~~damages aren't~~ **damage isn't** serious.
9 The ~~feedbacks~~ **feedback** from customers ~~have~~ **has** been almost entirely positive.

2 2 competition 3 paper 4 businesses 5 business 6 time 7 room 8 competitions 9 coffee 10 rooms 11 papers 12 times

3 2 – 3 The 4 a 5 – 6 A 7 a 8 the 9 the 10 – 11 the 12 – 13 a 14 – 15 The

Vocabulary

2 have offered/are offering 3 presented 4 donation 5 offer 6 share 7 presentation 8 donated 9 share

Unit 15

Vocabulary

1

Verb	**Noun**	**Adjective**
entertain	entertainment	entertaining
excite	excitement	exciting
attract	attraction	attractive
enjoy	enjoyment	enjoyable
protect	protection	protective
create	creation/ creativity	creative
appreciate	appreciation	appreciative
communicate	communication	communicative
co-operate	co-operation	co-operative
benefit	benefit	beneficial

2 2 co-operation 3 attractive 4 exciting 5 appreciation 6 creativity 7 protective 8 beneficial 9 enjoyable 10 communication

3 2 leader 3 meeting 4 player 5 effort

4 2 maintenance staff 3 management consultancy 4 suggestions box 5 quality control

Grammar

2 down 3 to 4 the 5 and 6 a 7 of 8 out 9 no 10 on

Unit 16

Grammar

1 2 several 3 many 4 a few 5 a great deal 6 a little 7 A great deal of 8 so many, very little

2 2 – 3 of 4 – 5 of 6 of 7 of 8 of 9 –, of

Grammar and vocabulary

2 B 3 A 4 B 5 B 6 C 7 A 8 B 9 A 10 C 11 C 12 C

Vocabulary

2B 3A 4B 5C

Unit 17

Grammar

2 *Sample answer*
In April, the unemployment rate stood at just over 8 per cent. *It increased slightly* in May but then it remained constant during the month of June. In July *there was a sharp rise* to over 10 per cent. From July to September, *it rose very gradually* but in October *there was a steeper rise* to reach 12 per cent. After that, however, *there was a gradual decline* until January. At this point it levelled off, but then *it dipped suddenly* to below 10 per cent in the month of March.

3 2 steady 3 strongly 4 recent 5 sharply 6 completely 7 unexpected 8 confident

Vocabulary

Company X

1 The share price rose slightly on Monday and continued …
2 … to climb the following day. However, …
3 … Wednesday saw an end to this upward trend as the price levelled off.
4 There were no further increases on Thursday either but unfortunately on Friday …
5 … the price suddenly plunged to just below Monday's value.

Company Y

1 The share price showed a slight fall on Monday and continued …
2 … to go down the following day. However, …
3 Wednesday saw an end to this downward trend as the price stabilised.
4 There were no further drops in price on Thursday either but on Friday there was a complete change of fortune as …
5 … the price suddenly recovered and rose sharply to exceed even Monday's value.

Unit 18

Vocabulary

1 2 5,940 3 750 4 810 5 7,540 6 6,100 7 840 8 1,000

2 1 total overheads 2 gross profit

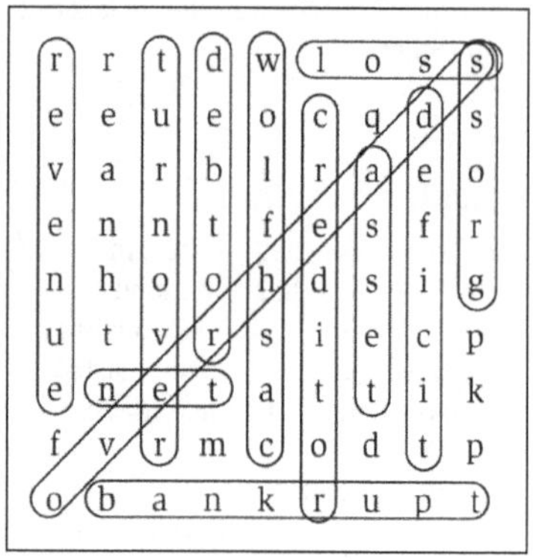

3 2 debtor 3 turnover 4 revenue 5 overheads 6 loss 7 bankrupt 8 gross 9 net 10 deficit 11 cashflow 12 asset

Unit 19

Grammar

1 In December people often feel positive about the New Year: 2; People are on holiday in July and August: 4; The stock market is influenced by many different things: 3; Big gains in share prices usually happen very suddenly: 1

2 2 because 3 so 4 However 5 because 6 so

Vocabulary

Across: 6 portfolio 8 bull 9 subsidiary 10 stake 11 flotation 12 merger 13 dividend

Down: 1 capital 2 returns 3 stock 4 commodities 5 broker 7 bonds 8 bear

Unit 20

Grammar

1 2 We are writing with regard to invoice number 931, which remains unpaid.
3 Yesterday I spoke to your colleague who told me to phone back today.

4 We are staying at a hotel on the Nile where Agatha Christie once stayed.
5 I saw a man on the train who looked just like your finance director.

2 2 which 3 who 4 which 5 which

3 2 playing board games
3 moral or religious board games
4 $50
5 'Banking'
6 $100
7 George S. Parker Company

Vocabulary

1 2 poured 3 took out 4 flood
5 back up 6 raise

2 2 took off 3 ride 5 crash 6 took off
7 headed for 8 ride 9 crash
10 headed for

Unit 21

Vocabulary

1

Adjective	Noun
punctual	punctuality
polite	politeness
rude	rudeness
generous	generosity
kind	kindness
sincere	sincerity
original	originality
reliable	reliability
creative	creativity
sensitive	sensitivity
loyal	loyalty

2 2 original, creativity
3 helpfulness, politeness
4 loyal, stability 5 sensitivity

3 2 g 3 a 4 f 5 d 6 b 7 h 8 c

Grammar

2 which 3 a 4 from 5 also 6 where
7 the 8 would 9 for 10 to

Unit 22

Grammar

1 2 e 3 d 4 a 5 b 6 f

2 2 were/was, would not/wouldn't ask, would/'d wait
3 do not/don't give, will/'ll do
4 spoke, would/'d start
5 offered, would/'d accept

Vocabulary

2 graduated
3 curriculum vitae (CV)
4 turned down
5 human resources
6 lay off
7 redundant
8 redundancy
9 graduate
10 curriculum vitae (CV)
11 social networking

Unit 23

Vocabulary

p	a	m	m	c	w	z	m	l	p	n	y	p
g	p	s	x	r	h	r	e	f	e	r	e	e
s	p	r	v	l	f	o	i	f	r	c	e	q
h	r	é	j	w	l	i	z	z	s	b	l	o
o	a	s	j	t	o	w	k	o	o	p	c	n
r	i	u	s	u	g	g	f	t	n	y	n	u
t	s	m	q	i	p	y	y	o	n	t	o	a
l	a	é	l	a	y	o	f	f	e	d	t	p
i	l	k	c	j	d	t	j	g	l	o	i	v
s	f	l	p	r	o	m	o	t	e	p	c	h
t	w	o	r	k	f	o	r	c	e	b	e	b
d	i	s	m	i	s	s	v	h	b	p	j	o
y	a	u	j	y	x	r	e	t	i	r	e	r
d	q	w	t	u	r	n	d	o	w	n	n	c

2 promote 3 lay off
4 workforce 5 shortlist 6 dismiss
7 referee 8 notice 9 appraisal
10 turn down 11 retire
12 personnel

Grammar

2 performance 3 management
4 interruptions 5 seriously
6 knowledge 7 criticism(s)
8 demotivated 9 improve
10 avoid 11 measure 12 promptly

Unit 24

Grammar

2 setting 3 to waste 4 to achieve
5 to become 6 trying 7 working
8 to complete 9 to break
10 achieving 11 to work 12 to make
13 to write 14 Putting

Vocabulary

2 high flier
3 perfectionist
4 star performer
5 team player
6 problem solver

Grammar and vocabulary

2 A 3 C 4 B 5 C 6 C 7 B 8 A 9 A
10 B 11 A 12 B 13 C 14 A 15 A 16 B

Writing supplement

Punctuation

Capitalisation

1 2 g 3 j 4 i 5 e 6 d 7 b
8 f 9 h 10 a

2 Hi Mark,
Just thought I'd drop you a quick email from Brussels. The visit to Hedex seems to be going well. My French isn't that good as you know but most of the directors here speak really good English. Hopefully, I'll come back with a definite order.
My hotel is really nice, quite near to Grand Place, which is very central.
I don't think I'll have time for much sightseeing but I saw the NATO headquarters from the taxi yesterday.
I'm catching the Eurostar back to London on Thursday so I'll give you a call that evening. Hopefully, we can meet up some weekend later in April.
Speak soon,
Rosemary

Apostrophes

1 2 e 3 c 4 a 5 d 6 f

2 2 We are one of **Europe's** largest holiday companies.
3 Browse our unique range of **ladies'** watches from our online store.
4 **Men's** shoes upstairs.
5 Your **company's** contact details will be included on our **members'** page.
6 *Correct*

Full stops and commas

1 2 c 3 b 4 d 5 a 6 f

2 1 Hi Franco
Just a note to say thanks so much for taking the materials to the Unifreight office last night. I know it was a long day for you and you wanted to get home so I really appreciate it.
2 Hi Jenny
I think your design for the flyers is great but we can't change them now because they have already gone to the printers. I will keep your design on file and maybe we can use it for the next batch.

3 The purpose of this memo is to record two conversations with Amanda Todd regarding her use of the office phone.
I first raised the issue with Amanda on 14 May. Amanda explained that she lived with her elderly mother who was in poor health. She said that she needed to check up on her during the day. I pointed out that she could use her mobile for this and that employees' use of the phone should be limited to work-related issues. However, the bill that I received after this conversation showed no reduction in the number of Amanda's phone calls.
In a meeting on 12 June Amanda said again that the calls were to her mother. She said that she could not use her mobile for this because the signal was not always clear. I told her that although we sympathise with her situation, we cannot accept this number of personal calls. As well as the cost, they take up too much of her work time. I also told her that if she does not reduce the number and length of these calls, we will have to issue her with a written warning.

Spelling

1 *er / or*
   2 distributor
   3 interviewer
   4 auditor
   5 supplier
   6 lawyer
   7 consumer
   8 shareholder
   9 plumber
   10 editor
   11 creditor
   12 visitor

2 *c / k / ck*
   2 *correct*
   3 gross domestic product
   4 a peak period
   5 *correct*
   6 *correct*
   7 a blank cheque
   8 publicity seeking

3 *ie / ei*
   2 brief
   3 receive
   4 grievance
   5 freight
   6 achieve
   7 height
   8 neighbour
   9 deceive
   10 receipt

4 **Doubling consonants**
   2 dropped
   3 heating
   4 contained
   5 happened
   6 auditing
   7 committed
   8 targeted
   9 profitable
   10 equipped
   11 reference
   12 transferred

5 **Suffixes and words that end in *e***
   2 packaging
   3 arrangement
   4 closely
   5 insurance
   6 machinist
   7 boredom
   8 generative
   9 unfortunately
   10 consumables
   11 safety
   12 advisable

6 **Silent consonants**

F	E	F	A	S	T	E	N	D	A
K	N	O	W	L	E	D	G	E	H
C	A	M	P	A	I	G	N	B	O
S	K	H	O	N	E	S	T	T	U
Q	G	M	X	Q	B	Z	O	Y	R
W	H	R	E	S	I	G	N	D	C
R	U	C	O	L	U	M	N	C	K
A	H	D	A	K	B	O	M	B	H
P	S	Y	C	H	O	L	O	G	Y
O	C	R	E	C	E	I	P	T	W

7 Dear Mr Anderson,
I am writing with *reference* to order 2547 which we *received* on 12 May. Although all the items were correctly listed on the invoice, *unfortunately*, the cutlery that we ordered was missing. Instead of cutlery, one of the crates *contained* a duplicate set of glassware. Please could you make *arrangements* to deliver the missing cutlery as soon as possible and let us know how we should return the second set of glassware.
Yours *sincerely*,
Hideko Miyoshi

Dear Ms Miyoshi,
We are sorry about the mistake in your order, which evidently *happened* at the packing stage. We have now dispatched the missing cutlery and we will arrange for one of our *distributors* to *pick* up the extra glassware within the next two weeks. We would be grateful if you could leave it in the original *packaging*. Once again, please accept our apologies for the inconvenience.
Kind regards,
Thomas Anderson

Writing fluently

Pronouns and reference words

1 2 them/these 3 they 4 him 5 this 6 one

2 2 service 3 date 4 policy 5 event 6 matter

3 *Suggested answer*

Dear Mr Wells,

I am writing with regard to payment for invoice 2581. According to our records we have still not received payment for this. I emailed you about this matter on 8 November and I also spoke to a member of your finance team the following week.

I would be grateful if you could make this payment as soon as possible and by 10 December at the latest. If we do not receive it by this date, we will be unable to supply you with further goods.

I enclose a copy of the relevant invoice for your reference.

Link words: contrasts

1 2 e 3 c 4 d 5 a

2 2 but 3 although 4 despite

3 *Whereas* follows the same rules as *although*.

4
- 2 Despite numerous telephone calls, (B)
- 3 Although I will certainly miss working here, (C)
- 4 but I hope to stay in contact with colleagues here (D)

Link words: causes, effects and purposes

1 2 C; E 3 C; E 4 E; C

2
- 1 This is because
- 2 so, This means that
- 3 so, because
- 4 This means that, This is because

3 in order to: an infinitive
so that: a phrase with a modal verb

4 *Suggested answers*
- 2 In order to make office communications clearer
- 3 so (that) I can contact you if there are any delays
- 4 This is because a number of accounts have been hacked.
- 5 as/because we want to make a good impression on our visitors.

Link words: addition

1 2 also 3 as well as 4 a before b after

2 2 and 3 also 4 As well as 5 and

3 2 A 3 B 4 C 5 C 6 B 7 A 8 B 9 B 10 C 11 C 12 A

Organising your writing

Beginnings and endings

1 2 B 3 E 4 B 5 B 6 E

2 2 e 3 d 4 a 5 f 6 b

Giving additional information

1 2 b 3 c 4 a

2 2 a 3 b 4 c

3
- A Re: your letter of 15 September. I am sorry to hear of the problems you have experienced with the new security system. We have arranged for our maintenance team to visit your office on 20 September to locate the error. We will also carry out a full check of the whole system. Once again, please accept our apologies.
- B I am writing with regard to your website which advertises second-hand office furniture. I am currently looking for five large filing cabinets. Please could you let me know if you have anything suitable in stock? I would also like to know if you can arrange delivery. I can be contacted on this email or on 07869 456734.

Paragraphing

1 2 b 3 a

2
- 2 True 3 True
- 4 False. This is one possible way of showing where a new paragraph begins (called *indentation*). The indentation does not have to be 3 cm. However, nowadays most business letters do not use this, and just leave a line space between paragraphs instead.
- 5 False. If you do this, you will confuse the reader about where the paragraphs begin and end.
- 6 False. Most paragraphs contain several sentences but business letters often begin and end with a one-sentence paragraph.

3 When Paolo Perri moved to London from Naples over ten years ago, there was one thing he missed. That was real

Italian ice cream. He couldn't find it in any of the local stores, so he decided to set up his own company. That was the beginning of Gelateria Perri.

Now we have grown from one single London shop to a company with over fifteen outlets. We have just opened our first outlet outside London, in the seaside town of Brighton. Not only that, but we supply our products nationwide to a number of key players in the hospitality industry.

Our ice cream is always made from fresh ingredients and contains no artificial flavourings. You will find our eight key flavours in any of our stores but we can also create flavours on request. As well as ice cream, we now produce a number of other popular frozen desserts.

To contact us, log on to sales@gelateriaperri.co.uk. Alternatively, drop into any of our ice cream stores. We are always willing to discuss your business needs and we take pride in our personal customer service.

4 *Suggested answer*
Paragraph 1: How we began
Paragraph 2: Distribution
Paragraph 3: Product details
Paragraph 4: Contact details/Contact us

5 Dear Sirs,
We at the Young Entrepreneurs Society are planning to hold an exhibition this summer and we are writing to ask if your company would be willing to sponsor a stand at this event.

The exhibition will be held on 25 July at the Park Hotel. It will provide an opportunity for our most promising young business people to present their services and products and, as a sponsor, your company would benefit from all the publicity for the event. We expect several thousand people to attend, including a number of well-known personalities from the business world. There will also be a programme of entertainment.

We have several different packages for sponsorship. Please find details on the sponsorship forms enclosed with this letter. We also enclose a brochure giving further information about our society and the work that we do.
We look forward to hearing from you and thank you in advance.

Yours faithfully,
Pat Samuda

6 Dear Ms Samuda,
Thank you for your letter giving details about the Young Entrepreneurs exhibition on 25 July. Unfortunately, I am afraid we are unable to sponsor the event at this time.

Your society clearly does very valuable work in encouraging and supporting young business people. Although our internal budget does not allow us to provide funding, a member of our management team would be delighted to attend the exhibition.

Please accept our best wishes for the success of the event.

Yours sincerely,
Donald Kantor